Praise from influential leaders who have endorsed *Inspired People Produce Results*

"Inspired People Produce Results *is full of simple truths that apply to everyone in a position of influence—managers, teachers, coaches, or parents. Let Jeremy Kingsley's words inspire you so you can inspire others—for the greater good.*"

Ken Blanchard,
Coauthor of *The One Minute Manager*

"*Jeremy's thoughtful analysis and perspective on the important role of inspirational leaders is long overdue. This easy-to-read book is sure to provide you with valuable insights to drive engagement levels and ultimately greater results in your enterprise.*"

David A. Binkley,
Senior Vice President, Global Human Resources,
Whirlpool Corporation

"*In a time when so much in business is uninspired and purposeless, how refreshing to find a book that talks about the importance of inspiration and of meeting the everyday needs of the talent that can take your business to the next level.*"

Andy Lorenzen,
Director of Organizational Effectiveness
Chick-fil-A, Inc.

"Business plans so often translate to sterile binders full of spreadsheets and data, and lead to labored, mechanical implementation. Jeremy Kingsley has chosen to focus on the most critical element often missing in companies—not instruction, but inspiration. He has laid out a practical framework to understand what makes for inspired teams and the critical role of leadership."

Micky Pant,
CEO,
Yum! Restaurants International

"Now is the perfect time for leaders to understand the importance of inspiring their team. Jeremy Kingsley has given us a tool to help accomplish that with Inspired People Produce Results. This book captures essential principles that will help you to help your people reach their personal and professional goals."

Richard L. Federico,
CEO and President,
P.F. Chang's China Bistro, Inc.

"Managers manage, but leaders must inspire! Jeremy teaches us nine fundamental yet critical items each of us must practice to inspire our teams toward success."

Tobin Cassels,
President,
Southeastern Freight Lines

"Leadership helps individuals find the meaning behind their professions beyond the financials, technologies, or the day to day process. Jeremy captures the key component in creating that meaning—inspiration—and then the building blocks necessary to make it a reality."

John A. Meyer,
Co-chairman and CEO,
Arise Virtual Solutions Inc.

"*Leadership is not just about developing the skills and strengths of your team, or placing employees in the right position, it's also learning what it takes to inspire people! Jeremy Kingsley has provided a book with vital principles to enhance your effectiveness as a leader so you can become a person that others will WANT to follow.* Inspired People Produce Results *is insightful, to the point, and a must read.*"

Dr. Hans Finzel,
President of HDLeaders,
best selling author of
The Top Ten Mistakes Leaders Make

"Inspired People Produce Results *is full of principles not only beneficial for business leaders, but for education leaders as well. It is full of practical insights that can be used to promote educational excellence in our schools. School administrators need to continually appraise methods they use to inspire and motivate their teachers. If PRINCIPALS can learn and apply the PRINCIPLES as presented in this book, they will be providing an environment for teachers that will consequently augment student learning.*"

Dr. Robert Pallone,
Former Education Specialist,
U.S. Department of Education

Inspired People
PRODUCE
RESULTS

Inspired People
PRODUCE
RESULTS

How Great Leaders Use
Passion, Purpose, and Principles
to UNLOCK Incredible Growth

JEREMY KINGSLEY

NEW YORK   CHICAGO   SAN FRANCISCO
LISBON   LONDON   MADRID   MEXICO CITY   MILAN
NEW DELHI   SAN JUAN   SEOUL   SINGAPORE
SYDNEY   TORONTO

1 2 3 4 5 6 7 8 9 10   DOC/DOC   1 8 7 6 5 4 3

ISBN 978-0-07-180911-5
MHID   0-07-180911-2

e-ISBN 978-0-07-180912-2
e-MHID   0-07-180912-0

Book design by Mauna Eichner and Lee Fukui

Library of Congress Cataloging-in-Publication Data

Kingsley, Jeremy.
  Inspired people produce results : how great leaders use passion, purpose, and principles to unlock incredible growth / by Jeremy Kingsley.
      p. cm.
  Includes bibliographical references.
  ISBN-13: 978-0-07-180911-5 (alk. paper)
  ISBN-10: 0-07-180911-2 (alk. paper)
  1. Leadership. 2. Inspiration. 3. Integrity. I. Title.
  BF637.L4K474 2013
  158'.4—dc23   2012036264

McGraw-Hill Education books are available at special quantity discounts to use as premiums and sales promotions or for use in corporate training programs. To contact a representative, please e-mail us at bulksales@mcgraw-hill.com.

This book is printed on acid-free paper.

This book is dedicated to leaders everywhere
who truly desire to make a difference.

Contents

Acknowledgments

I would like to express my deepest gratitude to my board of directors, (Reggie Boan, Russ Holt, Heather Matthews, Mark Nalepa, and Rick Toburen) for their continued support and encouragement. I would also like to thank James Lund for his valued partnership and help in bringing this project to life.

Introduction

I have been traveling full-time since 1995. I am a globe-trotter, a road warrior, an airport rat—all those labels you've heard for the frequent flyer and more. My wallet is filled with every rewards card from Hertz to Hilton. My friends at Delta Airlines treat me so well that they should be invited to my family reunion. Living out of a suitcase is not easy and not always fun. But traveling has presented me with some great experiences. In my career as an inspirational speaker, author, and consultant, I have had the opportunity to meet and work with amazing men and women—*leaders* in business, education, government, charities, churches, and other institutions. Many have incredible success stories— people who achieve excellence in their fields and make it possible for those around them to do the same.

As I've watched these men and women at the office, at sporting events, at restaurants, and in their own homes and observed how they relate to others, I've often wondered: *exactly what is it that makes a great leader today?*

If you're a leader yourself, or aspire to be, you may be wondering the same thing.

The modern manager deals with a very different world from the one managers faced just a generation ago. The pace of change in the workplace is staggering. New companies form and within weeks must expand, merge with another, or shift their emphasis to survive. Established companies that we consider bedrocks of the business landscape suddenly vanish (remember Lehman Brothers, Washington Mutual, and Sharper Image?). Technological advances in communication, production, delivery, and service cause us to run harder just to keep pace. If we're not four steps ahead, we're falling behind.

Then there is our unpredictable economy. The repercussions of the global recession that began in 2008 are still being felt today. The slow recovery has instilled fear of a second recession. How does a business leader know when or if to invest in research, hire new staff, or increase production when the market is so unstable? How can a manager have confidence in decisions based on constantly changing conditions?

Finally, there is the workforce itself. Most of today's employees aren't part of the loyal, hard-working group born between 1946 and 1964, the baby boomers. The younger workers, born between 1965 and 1994, have their own labels: generation X, generation Y, the millennial generation, or generation net. I call them "generation me." They are smart, optimistic, creative, and flexible, and thrive on diversity. Yet they are also known for a sense of entitlement, opinionated dialogue, and free-spending habits. They're looking for more than a job. They want a *relationship* with their boss and colleagues. They are used to working at their own pace. They don't like rigid schedules or long hours. And this one may be most important of all: when assigned a task, they often require more information. There's a crucial question they need to ask before they can start: Why?

Regardless of a staff member's age and attitude, the challenge for any leader is to get the most out of his or her people. The quality of interaction between boss and employee is critical. I've seen company directors who don't have the first idea of how to guide their staff. The result is confused, unhappy, and unproductive employees. Yet I've also seen bosses who lead their teams to surprising levels of success, with everyone actually enjoying the process.

The more I observed these differences, the more I began to ask myself, what is it that makes a great leader? How can today's boss thrive while directing a diverse team in a rapidly changing world? I used to think that the ability to lead was innate and, therefore, could not be learned. But I was fascinated by successful authority figures. I took notice each time I encountered individuals so charismatic, so clearly admired, so unforgettable, that *leader* might as well have been tattooed on their foreheads. I started an ever-growing list of these leaders and what they had accomplished. One day I decided to print it and read the entire thing.

As I read, something struck me. Most of these people believed in certain principles and possessed the same attributes. These principles and skills were recognizable and definable. I had a feeling that once all these things were identified and categorized, they could be passed on and learned by others. They could be a staircase, a step-by-step path to successful leadership.

To be an effective leader, however, I noticed that there is one step that stands out from the rest. If you don't get this one down, my guess is that you'll see only limited results from the others. I think it's the key that unlocks everything.

It's called *inspiration*.

Have you ever heard the phrase, "A manager is a manager"? The title is nice, and the respect that goes with being at the top of the team hierarchy is even better. Nevertheless, a manager is a manager. He or she will be obeyed for the most part. Instructions will be carried out, tasks will be completed, and projects will be brought to fruition. Work will be efficient, and that's about it.

A leader, on the other hand, *inspires*. I like the definition "to influence, move, or guide." Leaders motivate their team in ways team members never dreamed of. A leader welds hearts and minds together so that men and women function as one, achieving successes they'd never seen before.

Managers come and go, but a leader's influence is never forgotten.

Are you just a manager? Would you like to become an effective leader? Would you like to take your leadership to the next level? Would you like to learn how to inspire your team to success beyond its dreams and unlock incredible growth? I hope so because inspired people produce results.

What Do Leaders Do?
INSPIRE

If your actions inspire others to dream more, learn more, do more, and become more, you are a leader.

John Quincy Adams

Who has inspired you? Maybe your parents, a friend, a president? What did they do that had such an impact on you? I bet if you think back to your school days, you'll remember a teacher who inspired you. When I think back to one of my favorite decades, the eighties, one teacher sticks out in my mind: David First.

Some of the greatest leaders are teachers. I met a new group of them when I started my sophomore year of high school in the suburbs of Washington, DC. I had just transferred from a rival school. Needless to say, I faced a tough transition. Fortunately, starting at point guard on the varsity basketball team helped me gain some quick respect. For my junior year, I set some personal goals. I wanted to become class president, more popular, and have more friends among the "in crowd."

When the first day arrived, I was ready. I had on my Bugle Boy pants, the coolest T.J. Maxx shirt around (my wife might say that's debatable), and my untied high-top Filas. I watched for the people who would help make me the man of the moment. What I didn't know was that I was about to encounter a guy who would inspire me and help shape not only my year but my future. As classes began, there was a good deal of excitement. The talk was that a new teacher named Mr. First had joined the school faculty. People said he was a good-looking guy who might be a "cool teacher." Of course, we students would be the judge of that. When third period rolled around, I walked into his class wondering if he would live up to the hype.

He started with the typical formalities and then began to tell the story of how he ended up at this school in DC. Coincidentally, he made some big decisions during his junior year in high school. Following his high school graduation, he turned down a few offers to play lacrosse at well-known universities to compete in club lacrosse at a small college in Ohio. During his time there, he fought to figure out his purpose in life. At the end of this struggle, his pursuit led him to Columbia International University (CIU) in South Carolina. At CIU, he earned an undergraduate teaching degree and then landed his first job at our school.

From the day I met him, Mr. First captured my attention. Something was different about him. It was obvious that he meant everything he said; he wasn't fake. He was passionate about teaching. You could tell from a mile away that this guy cared about his students and believed that their lives could be changed for the better in the classroom.

More than 20 years later, I still remember the day Mr. First told us about his ski slope incident. He had stopped near the bottom of a run when a man in a blue jacket powered down the slope and literally ran him over, leaving Mr. First a crumpled mess. Mr. Blue Jacket didn't stop to say he was sorry or even check on the damage. He just continued skiing down the hill.

Just watching him retell the story in our classroom, you could see Mr. First's anger flare again. His eyebrows arched. He gritted his teeth. He told us that in that moment on the slope, he made it his mission to find Mr. Blue Jacket and show him what a *real* wipeout looked like. From my desk on the far right side of the room, I silently cheered him on: *Yeah! Go get him! Revenge!*

Mr. First went on. Later that day on the slope, from a distance, Mr. First saw Mr. Blue Jacket start a new run. Mr. First dug in his poles and chased after him. He didn't care about anything but catching this guy and teaching him a lesson. He was too far away until finally, at the bottom, Mr. Blue Jacket stopped and Mr. First had his chance. He plowed into him at full speed! He landed a powerful blow and sent the man flying facedown into the snow.

The satisfaction Mr. First felt vaporized, however, as soon as the man rose to his knees and turned around, *"Oh no,"* he thought. *"It's the wrong guy!"*

As he told the story, Mr. First's voice got very quiet. You could see on his face that he still felt ashamed and embarrassed.

"I blew it," he told us. "When somebody does something bad to you, I don't want you guys to respond like that. Revenge is not the way to handle a conflict."

It was great wisdom. I still try to apply that principle today when a struggle comes up with certain people in my life

who have hurt me in some way. The main reason why I remember that story and that moment, however, is that it
showed that Mr. First cared about us. He was willing to look
foolish and to be humble enough to share one of his mistakes
with his students if it would help guide us to a better future.
He was committed to helping us learn not just academic information, but also lessons on life.

Some people say that the best things you can share with
a person are the things you are most passionate about. Mr.
First did this every day.

That class was life changing. As the semester progressed,
I had opportunities to speak with Mr. First one on one. He
became my mentor. I asked him a ton of questions about life,
relationships, and future jobs he could see me doing. Since
my high school graduation was not far off, he mentioned his
alma mater down south and encouraged me to check it out.
One day I went home and said, "Dad, I'm going to South Carolina." After we talked and discussed the implications of the
decision, he agreed, and several months later I enrolled at
CIU. I earned my bachelor's and master's degrees there.

I have now lived in South Carolina for almost 20 years.
Though much time has passed, my encounter with David First
is one I will never forget. He was a leader who inspired me.

Thinking Like a Leader

If you are reading this book, you're probably a leader or ready
to become one. You may have held your job for a while, been
promoted recently, or are thinking ahead to an opportunity.

Whatever your situation, you have a desire to excel, to hone your skills, and to be effective in your position.

You may want to ask yourself: Do the employees know I care about them and their success? Does my team see me putting in the extra hours and effort needed to ensure excellence and results? Do team members sense that this is so important to me that I'm willing when needed to go over a project or product a second time, third time, or fourth time to make sure everything is exactly right? Can they hear in my voice the enthusiasm I have for who they are, what they're doing, and where we're going as a team and company? Your answers will show if you are a passionate leader or if you have work to do in this area.

We've talked about how some modern employees want to know the reasoning behind their duties. Blind, faithful obedience doesn't come naturally to them. They need to be motivated. They need to be *inspired*.

Have you ever received an e-mail from the boss saying something like, "*Janice, Ralph is running out of time to complete that Kramden report. I'm going to assign him to something else. Please clear your schedule to work on it and make sure that it gets finished by the end of the week*"? I have to admit, it's hard to get excited about such an assignment. The e-mail doesn't suggest why it's important in any way—certainly not important enough for Ralph to waste any more time on it. It doesn't sound like the boss will value the work. It feels more like a check-off-the-list task than an effort that will contribute to the company's success.

If you're ever the boss in this situation, why not take the extra time to say *why* it's important for Janice to finish

Ralph's report? Maybe Ralph is needed on another emergency situation. Maybe the report deadline has been moved up and Janice is known for efficiency and speed. If there's an opportunity to stress the value of and your appreciation for Janice's effort, put it in the e-mail. Even better, when possible, express it in person. You may be surprised to find Janice working twice as hard as she would have otherwise.

Wouldn't all of us like to leave the people around us with the ingrained desire to excel and be the best they can be? Of course we would, and we can. We can learn to be a source of inspiration. In our home and in our workplace, we can instill in others the conviction that work is a gift, that the task at hand is of primary importance, that the ability to carry it out is present, and that the job is worth doing supremely well.

We are human, however, and we cannot give what we do not have. In order to impart inspiration, we must possess it. Acquiring it is our first task.

Inspiration

Inspiration permeates our history and enriches our lives. It kept one man cramped and on his back, in the damp and the cold, for years while he painted the ceiling of the Sistine Chapel. It labored beside Sir Edmund Hillary and Sherpa Tenzing Norgay as they conquered the peak of Mount Everest for the first time. It sustained the passengers of a plane on that fateful day in September, strengthening them as they plotted their own deaths in a Pennsylvania field in exchange for the lives of others.

Inspiration! It is contagious. Yet only a fortunate few are born inspired. For most of us, this quality must be instilled in us before we can feel its spark. For managers, supervisors, or team leaders, the ability to inspire a group may be the most important attribute they can have.

A working division is composed of unique and disparate human beings who must, somehow, be combined into a smoothly functioning unit. For the division to perform at its best, each part has to operate at its optimum level in cooperation with the rest. It's like the human body. Eyes, ears, mouth, and brain all have unique characteristics and roles, yet their ability to work well and together is vital to the health and success of the body as a whole. If one part breaks down, the entire body suffers. It's the same for your team. Each employee must have a purpose, a willingness to achieve his or her best, and a commitment to helping the rest of the team do the same. Your task is to infuse into each employee the desire to fulfill that purpose to its utmost and to experience joy while doing it.

It comes from inspiration.

The poet Ralph Waldo Emerson once wrote, "Our chief want is someone who will inspire us to be what we know we could be." You can't buy inspiration like this at the supermarket. You won't find it on eBay. You must feel it before you can communicate it, and once you do, you can make it as infectious as an outbreak of the flu.

I heard a story about a group of great leaders, including industry giants, politicians, and top-ranking officers in the armed forces, that helped compile a list of qualities people needed to be considered effective leaders. They gave an interesting profile of the type of person these leaders look for when they have a management or team leader situation in mind. Let's take a look at the first few issues this group mentioned:

⇒→ **Do you connect with your company or corporation?** Do you absolutely believe in what your organization does and stands for? Are you proud of your product? Are you completely sure that, in your industry, your business is the best there is or is striving to become the best it can be?

Unless you believe these things, you will be unable to generate enthusiasm in your team. Football coaches lead their team in practice each week and then talk to their players in the locker room to get their players fired up on game day. You also spend your week preparing your team members to win on the field. On "game day," if you don't believe they have a chance for success, how will they believe it?

Research your company. Know it inside out. Be aware of professional accomplishments and discuss them, reminding your team that they can climb to even greater heights. Remember that younger employees tend to concentrate on the service side of business. What charities does your corporation support? Are you part of its fund-raising efforts? Do you encourage your team to participate? Giving back to the community can be a source of great satisfaction.

Generate and capitalize on that company spirit. You can use it to inspire others.

➤➤ **Do you have a plan for tomorrow?** Where do you see yourself in the corporate structure five or ten years from now? Have you built an effective team? Has your team risen with you? What have you accomplished along the way?

Part of plotting a clear path for your team is setting goals. And each goal should be a step toward the summit you aim to reach. You must keep it in sight at all times. Only you can decide how high or low this peak should be. Only you can establish the base camps you will need as you climb toward the summit. Think of your work as a journey toward your peak, and be aware that only a strong, united, inspired team can pitch those tents for you and secure them against inclement weather.

Give your team hope by choosing SMART goals: specific, measurable, attainable, realistic, and timely. Struggling for goals is fine, but attaining them invigorates your team and engenders new energy.

Keep your vision bright, and your team will follow its light.

➤➤ **Do you enjoy planning your strategy?** You should. It sharpens your skills and capabilities and stretches them to the maximum. Be fluid and able to change direction if necessary, but keep your goal in sight at all times. If you can see where you're going, it's much more likely your team will too.

Feeling inspired yet? Hang on. There's more.

➤➤ **Do you see the big picture?** It's easy to get bogged down in details, but someone has to see the whole picture, and that someone is you. Your vision is part of the long-range scenario, and so are your goals. You are the one with the map on which those goals are marked. You are your team's guide.

Keep your feet on the path, and those of your team members will follow.

➤➤ **Are you optimistic?** We've all heard the old question about whether the glass is half full or half empty. We've all heard it because it says a lot about us as human beings. Your glass should always be half full—you are doing the pouring. If your glass is emptying, your team's glass is doing the same. Tackle setbacks head on. See them as lessons, learn from them and use them positively. If you can avoid it, do not assign blame. Your staff members need to be held accountable, but use their mistakes as an opportunity to teach rather than punish. If you must discipline, do it right away in the teachable moment and do it in private.

An optimistic team has an optimistic leader.

➤➤ **Do you motivate others easily?** This is a key question. *Motivate* is a synonym for *inspire*. If you have dedication and loyalty, a vision and a plan for attaining them, a grasp of the entire concept of your plan or vision, and the positive confidence to implement it, then you are inspired, and you are ready to invigorate and unite your team.

Each of these traits is especially important. You can't assume that team members will follow you without question.

They expect to be filled in on the purpose of each step and how it fits into your plan for success. Work is more than a job to them. They want to find meaning in their activities.

You are the person to give it to them. All it takes is a little inspiration.

Fred the Postman

Mark Sanborn had just moved into an old house on a tree-lined street in a Denver neighborhood. When he heard a knock at his front door, he opened it and found a mailman standing there. "Good morning, Mr. Sanborn!" he said. "My name is Fred, and I'm your postal carrier. I just stopped by to introduce myself—to welcome you to the neighborhood and find out a little bit about you and what you do for a living."

Mark was surprised but impressed. He'd never received a personal visit from his postman before. He soon learned that a welcoming visit was only the beginning of the personal service that Fred provided. Fred always neatly bundled the mail in Mark's box. He made sure that no mail piled up when Mark was out of town—he held it for him without being asked. When a UPS package addressed to Mark was delivered to the wrong house, Fred carried it to its proper destination. One day, when Mark was mowing his front lawn, a familiar voice called to him, "Hello, Mr. Sanborn! How was your trip?" It was Fred, in his off hours, checking up on his "clients."

Mark, a professional speaker, began talking about his encounters with Fred to audiences across the country. They loved hearing about the postal worker who went out of his way each day to provide superior customer service. One discouraged worker who'd received no recognition from her employers wrote to Mark saying that Fred's example had inspired her to "keep on keeping on" and to continue doing what she knew was the right thing to do, even if no one noticed. A manager confided to Mark after a speech that he suddenly realized what his career goal was—to be a "Fred." Companies began establishing Fred awards to present to employees who mirrored the spirit of service and commitment displayed by the increasingly famous postal worker. One fan even sent Mark a box of cookies to give to Fred.

Fred's influence didn't stop there. Because of the enthusiastic response that Mark received whenever he talked about Fred, he decided to write a book about him and the principles he lived by. *The Fred Factor*, published in 2004, became a national bestseller.[1]

By simply trying to do a little extra and treating his customers as friends, a mailman named Fred inspired thousands across the country to do the same. If the example of a humble postal worker can have this kind of impact on people he didn't even know, your example as the leader of your team has the potential to provide even more inspiration.

Based on his experiences with Fred, Mark Sanborn offers four suggestions to those of us who seek to be Freds and inspire the people around us:

❯❯ **Inspire, but don't intimidate.** Fred isn't inherently extraordinary or superhuman. He's someone we can all relate to. He's an ordinary guy doing an ordinary job in an extraordinary way. Your behavior at work should be like this.

▶▶ **Involve.** Draw others into your efforts to encourage, serve, and inspire. A friend of Mark's once purchased and delivered a complete Thanksgiving dinner for a family that couldn't afford it. The next Thanksgiving, the friend invited Mark to join him in a similar effort, inspiring Mark to later invite others to help him serve those in need. When you involve others, your impact grows exponentially.

▶▶ **Initiate.** If you decide to wait for just the right moment, you'll be waiting a long time. To be a Fred, you must take bold and quick action. Be humble in your motives but not your example. When you initiate, you are the spark that lights a fire in others.

▶▶ **Improvise.** At an improv comedy show, the performers can take any situation and turn it into a funny scene. It's not the circumstances that determine the outcome but the participants. When your staff sees you keeping a positive attitude and trying new solutions even when everything's falling apart, they're likely to be inspired to rally around you.

Are you ready to be a Fred? Give it a try. You may find that it's just the example your team needs to reach new and extraordinary heights.

Influence Across Generations

Perhaps one of the most important effects of inspiration is its impact over time. When you motivate your staff members to do their best, you're doing more than raising the level of quality on a single report or project. You may be helping to establish a new attitude and approach that carries on for generations.

In the 1800s, a German named Hermann von Helmholtz made remarkable contributions to modern science, in particular in the fields of physics, physiology, and psychology. Helmholtz had a rare ability to see connections and possibilities. In physics, he is known for his theories on the conservation of energy and work in electrodynamics and chemical thermodynamics, as well as on a mechanical foundation of thermodynamics. In physiology and psychology, we remember him today for his insights into the mathematics of the eye, theories of vision, ideas on the visual perception of space, and research on color vision and the sensation of tone, perception of sound, and empiricism.

Helmholtz's legacy goes beyond these advances, however. His work with sound frequencies helped inspire Alexander Graham Bell's invention of the telephone. Helmholtz also taught a number of students, one of whom included the brilliant American physicist Henry Rowland. Rowland, in turn, instructed physicist and inventor Robert W. Wood, who wrote the textbook *Physical Optics*. A boy named Henry Land was fascinated by the 1915 edition of Wood's work, reading it "like the Bible." Land was inspired by Wood's descriptions and theories on polarization and became intrigued with the idea of developing stronger headlights for cars while controlling glare through polarization. After enrolling at Harvard, Land dropped out to continue his research. He later returned to Harvard, his work so impressing Harvard staff that he was given his own laboratory.[2]

Today, Henry Land is better known as an entrepreneur, as the inventor of instant photography, and as the creator of the Polaroid camera and corporation. In 1972, he made the covers of both *Time* and *Life* magazines.

This multigenerational story does not end with Henry Land. An inventor/entrepreneur patterned his career after Land, so admiring him that he said, "The man is a national treasure. I don't understand why people like that can't be held up as models: This is the most incredible thing to be—not an astronaut, not a football player—but *this*."[3]

The admirer was Steve Jobs. It was a sad day when he died on October 5, 2011, after a long struggle with pancreatic cancer. He was cofounder and CEO of the computer giant Apple, cofounder of Pixar animation studios, and codeveloper of the iMac, iTunes, iPod, iPhone, and iPad. Like Land, Jobs was a visionary who gave up college to pursue his dreams, was a perfectionist who disdained market research, built a multi-billion-dollar corporation around his inventions, and used shareholders meetings for dramatic introductions of new products.[4]

The list of people Steve Jobs has inspired is endless. He has been described as a pioneer and genius in the fields of business, innovation, technology, and product design. Various organizations have named him "the most powerful person in business,"[5] "CEO of the decade,"[6] and the "greatest entrepreneur of our time"[7, 8] for his influence on technology and the entertainment and music industries.

Jobs's vast contributions did not appear out of thin air. They are the continuation of a line of inspiration that stretches back to Henry Land, Robert Wood, Henry Rowland, Hermann von Helmholtz, and beyond. Don't underestimate the potential of your own efforts to inspire your team. You may find that you are influencing the work of visionaries for years—or even centuries—to come.

Insights for Inspiration—and Results

▶▶ For any leader, the ability to inspire may be the most important attribute.

▶▶ Many of today's employees require work that is meaningful.

▶▶ Know your organization and its strengths. Consistently point them out to your staff to build company spirit.

▶▶ Plan for the future. Set SMART goals for your team: specific, measurable, attainable, realistic, and timely.

▶▶ Adopt the traits of inspiring leaders: dedication, loyalty, vision, a commitment to planning, and confidence.

▶▶ Recognize that inspiration can leave a legacy for generations.

What Inspires People? 2
>>> PASSION

If you want to build a ship, don't herd people together to collect wood and don't assign them tasks and work, but rather teach them to long for the endless immensity of the sea.

Antoine de Saint-Exupery

How far will you go for something you are passionate about? How far will you drive to watch your favorite sports teams? How nice a diamond necklace will you purchase for your wife? How much cash will you throw down for the newest and greatest golf clubs? Many things in our lives tend to win our affection. Sometimes we even consider certain niceties as necessities. In my case, I must confess that Coca-Cola is an object of my focused desire.

Many people believe, sadly, that Coke is just another soft drink. I, however, have come to see its beauty as a complex concoction of liquid perfection. The taste of that sweet carbonated beverage sends my senses into a satisfied bliss. Could there be a finer drink that produces such savory sensations? For a long time, the color red has shown brightly from the bottom shelf of my fridge. I like to refer to this portion of the refrigerator as the "red zone." I prefer to make grocery trips for "the red" and the bread instead of milk and bread.

Many of my friends have also developed this liquid passion. We consistently eat only at restaurants where Coke is served. On certain days, we will even pass up a juicy steak dinner at a fine establishment that does not serve Coke for a lesser meal with an ice-cold Coca-Cola. If we are forced to grab dinner at a wayward restaurant that doesn't serve Coke, then we just stop at a gas station to purchase a bottle and get permission to bring it into the dining area. Some people might consider this obsessive. They are probably right. My friends and I do not stand alone, though. An entire Coke museum thrives in Atlanta, Georgia, just three hours west of my hometown. I know because I've been there!

I find it interesting that so many people who have seen and experienced my passion for Coke now have developed a little passion for "the liquid of heaven" themselves. After reading this, you may want a Coke. Did you know that passion can be contagious? Let's be clear. If you are a leader and you want to inspire your team members, they must see your passion.

A man named Bill was a publishing house editorial director. Bill viewed his position as much more than a job. This guy *loved* reading and talking about books. He deeply enjoyed the process of developing new book ideas and of guiding editors as they refined a manuscript. You could hear it in the rise and fall of his voice and see it in his smile when Bill talked—which was often—about a book he was excited about. In the shower, driving to work, and on weekends on his fishing boat he thought about titles and what would most effectively describe a book's message and attract potential readers.

Bill's employees caught his enthusiasm. During meetings, he interrupted discussions about editorial direction to comment on other books. He might ask, "Have you read Cormac McCarthy's new book? What did you think of it?"

You might consider that wasted time. I disagree. Bill was planting the seeds of passion in his team members. His staff looked forward to meetings, not just because they were an opportunity to develop project strategies, but also because they were often fun, enlightening, and energizing. Bill's passion for books and the process of producing books was contagious.

We talk about passion all the time, but few of us apply it to our job. Shouldn't we, though? We spend almost as much time with our colleagues at work as we do with our families (and in some sad cases even more). Out of each 24-hour period, we sleep for around 8 hours, commute to work, put in at least another 8 hours on the job, journey home, and enjoy what little time remains with our spouse and children (if that's what we return home to).

Many of us make a definite distinction between home and work. We would die to protect our family. We feel this passion without questioning its depth. But the other part of our lives, the working part, can be something else entirely. We want to do well because it means a promotion and a raise, and this makes life better for our family, but many of us are not really passionate about our work or about the colleagues with whom we spend so much of our time.

We should be. Without passion for this integral part of our lives, we are sleepwalking through our days for the sake of the paycheck we receive. With passion, however, our self-respect and sense of self-worth grow, and we have more to give both at work and at home.

I encourage you to look at each of your work projects with passion, with a sense of discovery and adventure. Explore the possibilities, implications, and ramifications. Relish the challenges. Greet them with the same passion you would a best friend from college you hadn't seen in years. If you feel it, your team will, too.

The Purpose of Passion

A survey of more than 7,000 U.S. workers found that only 45 percent of workers say they are satisfied or extremely satisfied with their jobs. "At the same time, a much lower number actually feel very 'engaged' by their jobs. Only 20 percent feel very passionate about their jobs; less than 15 percent agree that they feel strongly energized by their work; and only 31 percent (strongly or moderately) believe that their employer inspires the best in them."[1]

The vast majority of members of the U.S. workforce do not feel passionate about what they do and do not feel inspired by their bosses. You can be a different kind of leader, one that inspires passion. Here are just a few of the reasons why passion in the workplace is so important:

➤➤ Passion intensifies our focus.

➤➤ Passion enables innovation and creativity.

➤➤ Passion provides the drive to persevere, to avoid cutting corners, and to pursue excellence.

➤➤ Passion creates energy among colleagues that allows work to be completed more quickly.

➤➤ Passion helps people deal with fear.

➤➤ Passion makes employees want to stay in their jobs and contribute even when they're not feeling their best.[2]

Communicate your vision; make everyone around you see, taste, and feel it. Make it irresistible. Use words and pictures. Use music. Move as you speak. Do not stop until each team member is inspired and filled with the desire to make the dream a reality.

Before I speak to an audience, I always remind myself of an important rule: Be a novel, not a newspaper. Newspapers are usually thrown away the next day. Novels may be reread and cherished for years. When I speak, people want more than newspaper headlines. They want to know more than the basic facts. They want principles and stories that touch their five senses and emotions. They want to *experience* what I'm saying.

The same is true of your staff members. If you want them to understand and catch your passion, you've got to give them more than the facts. Tell them the story behind your excitement, and they'll begin to latch onto your vision.

As you describe your vision, take care to explain exactly how the dream can be fulfilled. If your team does not clearly see how this can be done, the dream is merely smoke. Invite participation. You want your team to begin to think as one, with each member having input. When everyone is sharing ideas, brainstorming, seizing on thoughts and theories, and conceiving ways to put them into practice, you will have succeeded.

Your team will have been inspired.

Study your team members. Find for each of them a niche, a venue that best fits their strengths, skills, and personalities—that one place that will ignite the fire of passion whose flame is inspiration. Bruce Woolpert, CEO of Granite Rock, a construction materials supplier in northern California, accomplished this through what he called the "Try-a-Job" program. It allowed any company worker to try his or her hand at a different company job for a day. A few employees even shadowed Woolpert in his role as company head. Another program gave employees promoted into new positions a 30-day trial period. During that time, if they didn't like their new job, they could go back to their old one, no questions asked.[3] People are excited about coming to work when they know they have the opportunity to move up, try new things, and discover where they can make their greatest contributions.

This is exactly what happened at Kahler Slater, a small architecture company in Milwaukee, Wisconsin.

"Years ago," says Jill Morin, one of three CEOs of the firm, "we noticed that when our employees were doing work they were passionate about, our clients benefitted because they got to work with highly motivated and enthusiastic people. The staff benefitted because they were working on projects that excited them."

Morin and her fellow executives decided to pursue company passion with, well, passion. They sat down with employees to specifically identify what got them excited at work. Then they devoted nearly a year to establishing a fresh business vision that incorporated everyone's mutual passions. The result was new business teams and new definitions of the type of clients the company sought to serve. Several employees, for example, said they wanted to be involved in projects that promoted healing, so the firm launched a healthcare team. Other employees reported a desire to move beyond the company's core brick-and-mortar business. They were given the opportunity to participate in a new focus on multimedia design.

The commitment to passion changed the bottom line at Kahler Slater. An increase in repeat business (greater than 90 percent annually) led to more work and greater profits, which were reinvested in the staff. "Supporting this passion," Morin says, "quickly became a key business strategy."

The following five tips reveal how Kahler Slater aims to ignite or reignite workplace passion among company employees. They can work for you too.

➤➤ Ask potential new hires what they're passionate about and how they can apply that passion to the work they want to do for the organization. A woman who interviewed for an executive assistant position at Kahler Slater responded to the passion question by calling herself a "neat freak." She described her joy in keeping things organized and under control. She became the assistant of a creative but rather unorganized executive at the firm.

⇒➔ Give employees the opportunity to share what they're passionate about. Kahler Slater periodically holds "creativity fire drills." Near the end of a workday, staff members are asked to pin up whatever it is they're working on and excited about. They talk about what is inspiring them, which then leads to new ideas and renewed enthusiasm among the rest of the team.

⇒➔ Provide time for passion to take root and grow. All Kahler Slater staff members are required to record at least nine hours of "creativity time" each year. One employee, for example, enrolled in a food styling course. The intent is for employees to use the time as they like to keep their creative juices flowing.

⇒➔ Support passions even if they aren't related to work. Families are a primary passion for many employees. Kahler Slater staff members are allowed to work from home or on flexible schedules. Some even bring their children to the office occasionally. The company attitude is, "An employee who is sitting at his desk fretting that he's missing his daughter's basketball game is most likely pretty unproductive at that moment. As long as the work gets done and the needs of clients and fellow team members are met, we trust our employees to honor their commitments at work while they're keeping their commitments at home."

➤➤ Relax. No one is passionate about something every moment of the day. It's vital to take the time to recharge
and renew, whether it's a spontaneous gathering of
staff, a holiday celebration, or a ceremony that honors
an important company milestone. Passion needs time
and attention to grow.[4]

Will all this emphasis on cultivating your passion lead
your staff away from your firm? Sometimes. Since the "passion program" was initiated at Kahler Staler, a number of
employees have moved on to launch new businesses in architecture, graphic design, and consulting. One even opened
a bakery and coffee shop. But the benefits of encouraging
your team members to embrace their passions far outweigh
these losses. Even when employees leave, positive word of
mouth and referrals may negate the sting of losing a worker.

Engage Your Team

How else can you encourage passion at work? Engage your
team members as much as possible. They will respond and
give in the same measure. Meetings will become energized
interchanges of ideas, each one sparking off another. The respect one team member shows for one another will grow,
and so will their respect for you.

Then, as things progress, take the time to point out and
praise each victory. Being congratulated for interim achieve-
ments motivates people and moves them on to the next challenge. Begin each meeting or gathering on a positive note,

pointing out the progress that has been made. Use visuals so that your team can see what it has accomplished and be eager to reach the next goal.

One other thing—be humble. If you want to see your passion go to waste, just walk around like you own the earth. No one wants to see, listen to, or work for an arrogant person. On the other hand, people respond to leaders who don't think too highly of themselves. You can be confident in your position and in who you are without having to broadcast it every day. Of all the passionate leaders I have come across, those who are humble often have the most loyal followers. Don't lead only as a professional; lead as a person.

Are you beginning to get the point? Passion can change your life! At work, your intense enthusiasm for a new venture will spread to others and make it seem possible. Instead of longing for the end of the day, you may start wishing that the day was longer. Are you catching the inspiration thing?

So what have we learned so far? That inspiration is vital to opening our visionary senses and allowing us to identify a dream, and that our passion for that dream inspires others and creates a passionate and enthusiastic team. Finding the best use of each person's talents helps ensure that he or she will excel. Liberal congratulations showered on workers as each phase is achieved keeps everyone motivated and headed for the goal. Make humility a cornerstone of who you are as a person and live it in your profession.

When passion is one of your leadership priorities, you will soon find yourself working with an inspired team.

Insights for Inspiration—and Results

➤➤ Most workers do not feel passionate about their jobs or inspired by their bosses. To inspire your staff members, you must show them your passion.

➤➤ To infuse passion, explain the story and vision behind your project.

➤➤ Give your team members opportunities to try and discover new things. Help them find the best uses of their talents.

➤➤ Celebrate victories. Point out the progress your people make.

➤➤ Mix humility with passion to inspire loyalty.

What Inspires People?
PURPOSE

3

As strong as my legs are, it is my mind that has made me a champion.

Michael Johnson

What a champion Michael Johnson was! Before he retired from competitive racing in 2000, Johnson garnered world records in the 200 meters, 400 meters, and 4 × 400 meter relay, and he ran the fastest 300 meters of all time.

Johnson won five Olympic gold medals and was crowned world champion nine times. He was the only male sprinter in history to win both the 200 and 400 meters events at the same Olympics, the Atlanta games in 1996, and the only man to successfully defend his title in the 400 meters at a summer Olympics competition.

Johnson's running style defied the contemporary perception that a high knee lift is essential for maximum speed. He was nicknamed "The Duck" because his head bobbed back and forth when he ran, his back was straight, and he did not use much arm drive. A reporter once asked, "If you had a usual running technique, like other runners, do you think you would go faster?"

"If I ran like all the other runners, I would be back there with them," Johnson replied.

Regardless of how he actually ran, Johnson's mind made him a champion. He knew where he was going—right to the front of the pack. His mind stayed focused on his goal, and his legs followed along.

After he retired from competitive sports, Johnson set new goals. He has worked as a television sports commentator, often for the British Broadcasting Company. He has written a column for the *Daily Telegraph*. Jeremy Wariner, who won the gold medal in the 400 meters at the 2004 Athens Olympics, employs Johnson as his agent.

Michael Johnson has an ongoing sense of purpose, a motivation that has carried him to the head of the pack and made him a winner in sports and in his later careers.

When Purpose Means Life or Death

A sense of purpose is vital to the success of an individual or a team. Sometimes it means the difference between life and death.

When several members of a Uruguayan rugby team survived a plane crash in the Andes mountains in 1972, they originally believed that rescue parties would find them. Then they heard on a radio that the search had been abandoned. Some of these young men lost hope at that point. They expected to die in the mountains, far from their family and homes.

A few of the survivors, however, focused not on the horror of their predicament but on a chance to escape. One of these was 22-year-old Nando Parrado, who talked repeatedly of climbing out of the mountains toward Chile and civilization. He could think of nothing else.

Nando's words provided purpose for the group. They began planning for a three-person trek, setting aside supplies and creating a makeshift sleeping bag and snowshoes. The preparations lifted everyone's spirits, giving them hope and energy to contribute to the effort.

Finally, Nando and two teammates set out to find help. One had to turn back, but Nando and his friend Roberto Canessa persevered. Their commitment and desperation propelled them forward when a single slip on the mountain slopes would have sent them to their doom. Nine days after beginning their climb, they encountered a hill-country peasant. Soon after, the remaining 15 survivors were rescued.

A sense of purpose allowed these terrified young men to achieve the "impossible." It will also allow your team members to stretch themselves beyond what they can imagine.

A Culture of Purpose

As the leader of your team, you must clearly understand and be able to pass on the purpose of your organization and your team's role within that organization. If you don't know the purpose of your efforts, you certainly won't be able to inspire your team to success.

Communicating purpose will take more than requiring your team to memorize the company mission statement, however. It must become part of the culture of what everyone in your organization thinks about, says, and does each day. It will influence decisions made at the top and choices made by the lowest-level employee.

Take, for example, Southwest Airlines. Founded in the 1970s, Southwest set out to make the airways affordable for everyone and "set the customer free." In a practical sense, this meant focusing on the priorities that supported the company's purpose—safety, airplanes, people, and airport locations—and not trying to match the standards of other airlines in other areas. The airline didn't provide the same meals, offer the same first-class amenities, or move customers through lines as quickly, and they were criticized for it. But founder Herb Kelleher said, "I'm in the business of democratizing the skies. I can't do it if we have high costs. If something increases our costs, we'll have to increase our fares, and we'll violate the purpose of the airline: democratizing the skies."[1]

The employees at Southwest Airlines knew their company's purpose and stayed focused on goals that promoted that purpose. This is especially important for today's younger employees who want to understand the process before they can fully engage.

I experienced this myself a few years ago. Compassion International, a nonprofit organization that promotes physical, emotional, and spiritual health for impoverished children around the world, was interested in having me speak across the country on its behalf. I'd heard good things about the organization, so I accepted the invitation to visit Honduras and observe what Compassion was doing there.

I wasn't prepared for what I saw. At a garbage dump in Honduras, I encountered families of up to 10 people living in 1-room, 12-by-12-foot shanties of loosely constructed tin and boards. They had no electricity or bathroom. A fire pit in the ground doubled as their stove and source of heat. The adults worked 10-hour days to earn their food for the day—two tomatoes. When a garbage truck pulled up to dump a new load of trash, hundreds of people emerged from the shanties to sort through the debris looking for anything useful.

I remember seeing a tiny one-year-old lying on a mattress in one of these shanties. My son Jaden was about the same age at the time.

"That little boy and his father could just as easily be Jaden and me," I thought.

When I learned of Compassion International's plans to help build a school in the area and provide food and clothes for the children, I was hooked. Compassion was making a difference here. I couldn't wait to give my first speech and get people excited about what was happening. I understood the plan. Suddenly, I understood purpose.

A Teaspoon of Purpose

Once a team knows where it is headed and is filled with the desire to get there, purpose keeps it on course. It is reborn at the opening of each week—and as the leader of your staff, it starts with you. Everyone needs a teaspoon of purpose in their Monday morning coffee, and you are there to dispense it.

You have plenty of methods at your disposal for consistently promoting purpose among your people. Become a sheepdog. Find any drifters, people with a puzzled look as they stare at their monitor or bend over a set of plans. Make time for them. Find out what is wrong. Redirect them. Restate their purpose and deal with any snags that have occurred. Get them back on course.

Keep that team together and keep it moving!

Keep your own sense of purpose honed and sharp. You are the leader. Keep that big picture in mind and know exactly where you are and where you are going. Communicate your enthusiasm and dedication. Carry everyone else along with you. It will take energy and effort, but no one said that being a leader was easy.

Grow together. At times, it may seem that everyone has a different purpose, and that paths are diverging. Don't forget that if you don't define your team's purpose, team members will, and what they come up with may not match what you had in mind. This can lead to internal conflicts and battles between departments; as a result, your business will suffer. On the other hand, when the team members are on the same page, decisions and strategy are filtered through your purpose. There should be a growing confidence that good results are near. Make sure that all team members see the way back to the common goal and that the impact their work will have on it is clear to them. It is as if each team member must make a brick, ensuring that it is strong and free from flaws. It must then be firmly set in place, among the other bricks, so that the next row can rest safely upon it.

Legs ache halfway through a race, and heads often ache at the same point during a challenge. It is purpose that carries tired limbs and overburdened minds on until a second wind comes and the finish line is in view. Purpose fathers that final burst of energy that carries your team over the line, with the broken tape fluttering in the wind.

Purpose paves the way to victory.

Define Your Unique Purpose

Your ability to inspire your staff may depend on your skill at defining your team or your company's unique purpose. Everyone wants to make more money and deliver better quality and service. Do you know what purpose separates you from the rest of the pack? Employees will quickly sense when a leader is pretending to have a plan or is settling for the same goals everyone else makes. It's your commitment to see beyond the routine and understand what's truly needed that will impress and motivate your people.

Let me explain what I mean. The people who make Porsche automobiles have a little secret. They don't measure up to their competition—except, apparently, where it counts the most.

A few years ago, *Car and Driver* magazine compared a new Corvette with the Porsche 911. The Corvette won in nearly every category. It was faster from zero to sixty, faster over a quarter mile, and faster to stop. It performed better on the skid pad. And the Corvette cost about 38 percent less than the Porsche 911. Despite these obvious differences, more than 30,000 supposedly sane North Americans purchased a Porsche instead of a Corvette that year, spending *$1.8 billion*. Porsche is a popular, well-marketed brand—but not that popular. So what gives?

According to the business experts who wrote *The Big Moo*, Porsche excels at a hard-to-measure, rarely discussed attribute called "path accuracy." The car goes exactly where drivers want it to go, giving them a sense of complete control. Drivers like that feeling—a lot. Porsche succeeds because it delivers on a unique goal—giving its customers the driving experience they want even though most of them would never be able to explain it. Porsche's leadership has a well-defined purpose that brings satisfaction to its loyal fans and profits to its investors.[2]

Sometimes defining your unique purpose means doing more with less. When Apple introduced the iPod, it quickly dominated the market. Then competitors threatened Apple's position by introducing inferior music players at cheaper prices. Would Apple respond by holding firm on the higher-priced iPod, likely leading to a downturn in sales, or would it compromise by offering a lower-quality version at a more affordable price?

The answer was neither. Apple identified a new purpose for its music technology brand. It created the iPod Shuffle. Unlike the regular iPod, the Shuffle had no screen, was less than a third the size of its predecessor, and was smaller than anything the competition offered. Most important, the Shuffle didn't store all of a customer's music. It stored some of it and played it back randomly, like a radio station that keeps playing your favorite songs. The Shuffle was cheaper than the iPod yet offered a unique service. Customers loved it and kept Apple at the forefront of the industry.[3]

ING Direct brought a similar approach to the banking industry. Over a three-year period, ING did not offer checking, had no ATMs, and didn't handle cash. It required no account minimums and didn't charge fees. It didn't have branches or tellers. It had no credit card or telemarketing programs.

What, you ask, *did* ING offer? Two things: actual human beings, not computers, who talk to you when you contact them. And higher interest rates.

The public responded to this strategy. During those three years, ING signed up more than 1 million new customers. An astonishing 40 percent of ING's new business came from referrals. That allowed the company to spend less on advertising and attract customers for a third of what a traditional bank spends.[4]

ING's directors had found their unique purpose. They cut out services and programs that many customers didn't care about and focused on what they wanted to do well. They invented a bank in which giving people less worked better.

What does all this mean for you? Simply that if you are a manager who is willing to think outside the box to define your team's unique purpose, your staff members will notice and buy in enthusiastically. They'll understand that you are an innovative leader with a plan for the present and the future. They will be inspired.

Linking Passion to Purpose

"Good leaders," it's been said, "create an organization with a purpose that rises above the bottom line; great leaders go a step further, finding ways to leverage the passion of each employee in order to create incentives that transcend financial rewards."[5]

What does this statement mean? I think it's saying that to be an exceptional leader, you must discover ways to link the passions of each individual on your team with the purposes of your organization. It often requires going beyond traditional methods.

Sometimes the link is easy. Trudy Novicki, for example, works for a nonprofit in Miami called Kristi House, which provides support and services for sexually abused children. She spent three decades as a prosecutor for the state attorney's office before she realized that her true passion was child advocacy.

Novicki believes that many people who are unhappy in their jobs either don't enjoy what they do or don't see a purpose in it. At Kristi House, she enjoys her work and feels that her work has purpose. The people she works with are equally devoted to their jobs.

"We say that it's our mission to end the epidemic of child abuse in Miami-Dade County," she says. "To have a goal like that gives a lot of purpose to your life."[6]

If your team hauls garbage for a refuse company or makes floor mats for cars and trucks, the goals of your organization may not seem as altruistic as advocating for victims of sexual abuse. But it's important to remind your team that there is value in any service.

Even more effective may be the practice of donating a percentage of your company's profits to a worthy cause. Many of today's employees seek meaning in every aspect of their lives. They'll be much more excited about their work if they know they're contributing toward better housing and schooling for disadvantaged families and children, toward meals for the homeless, or toward water wells for impoverished communities in Africa. It adds significance and purpose to their work that goes beyond material gain for themselves and your company.

As you get to know the members of your team, you'll discover more about their individual desires and goals and how they define their purpose in life. It may be based on their family values, faith, or recent experiences. Pay attention to these clues! The more you can find common ground between your organization's goals and purposes and the individual goals and purposes of each member of your team, the more effective and happy they will be on the job.

You won't regret making purpose a priority. It will make all the difference for you and your team, enabling the "impossible" to become the achieved.

Insights for Inspiration—and Results

➤→ Once a team knows where it is headed and is filled with the desire to get there, purpose keeps it on course.

▶→ Define and clarify the purpose of your organization, your staff, and each project for every member of your team.

▶→ Start each week by identifying purpose for your employees and instilling inspiration and energy in them.

▶→ Commit to defining your team and company's unique purpose.

▶→ Look for ways, no matter how unconventional, to link the passions of each individual on your team with the purposes of your organization.

▶→ Inspire your people by donating a percentage of profits to worthy causes.

What Inspires People?

→ LOYALTY

> *An ounce of loyalty is worth*
> *a pound of cleverness.*
>
> Elbert Green Hubbard

Every one of us has probably hoped to develop a loyal relationship at some point in life. We wanted to find and maybe did discover another person who would stick by our side through tears, careers, laughter, changes, and growth. We wanted a friend we could trust. We wanted to know that setbacks and arguments wouldn't easily break or disturb what we had built. Most of us, when we found this loyal person, described this rare relationship as *friendship*. Thankfully, I have had the opportunity to experience this special expression of loyalty.

As a young boy growing up in a small Midwest community, I met a guy in elementary school named Matt. From the start, I knew our relationship would be something special. Early on, I discovered an exciting route that led from our school to his house. I would cut across the cornfield behind the school and ride my skateboard down the hill into town, arriving at his house in 15 minutes flat. Matt and I loved sports, Star Wars, the Beach Boys, Tombstone pizzas, and the Atari 2600. One could make the argument that we liked girls too, but it's not like they were as important as Frogger. We mainly spent our time playing, talking, exploring, and as all good boys do, skateboarding.

As our friendship grew stronger, Matt and I decided we needed to make a pact of loyalty. Since we had become mature fifth graders, we understood the serious nature of this act. It would be an official declaration. It would stand as a mark of commitment and total allegiance, one to the other. So we decided to go all the way; we would carry out the ultimate handshake and become "blood brothers." The memory makes me smile to this day (although this would be frowned upon nowadays).

We developed a plan. First of all, under no circumstances would we tell anyone, especially our parents. Our bold move had to remain top secret. No one would ever know. Secondly, we decided to carry out the plan on a Wednesday night after church while my parents did their routine visitation with all their friends. We would sneak outside, climb into the back seat of the Kingsleys' huge 1982 Bonneville, find the paring knife that I would have secretly hidden under the seat, and do the deed under the moonlight.

When the night came, everything went as planned. We were alone in the dark parking lot. Nothing could stop us. Yet there was one problem. To become blood brothers, there must be blood! Did we really want to make an incision on our thumbs and draw blood for a special handshake just to show our loyalty?

After what seemed like hours of consideration, we decided to do it. It took about 20 attempts before either one of us could get even a tiny drop of blood. Maybe we had tough skin. Or maybe we were just a tad scared to slice our own fingers. Finally though, we both drew a little blood. So we put our thumbs together for the ultimate handshake. We were officially blood brothers! Together, we proved our loyalty.

Sadly, that spirit of deeply felt loyalty is frequently absent today. Husbands and wives routinely divorce one partner and take up with another. Professional athletes switch teams so often you need a scorecard to keep track of your favorite players.

It's the same in the modern workplace. Generations past expected to join a company and devote the rest of their working lives to making that organization as strong as possible. In return, they knew they could count on a steady paycheck and, after 30 or 40 or 50 years, a gold watch and pension plan. They showed loyalty to the company, and in return, the company took care of them.

Times have changed. Businesses appear and disappear at a dizzying pace. So do jobs. Technology has helped make our skills more versatile and applicable to multiple fields. People no longer expect to spend their working lives with the same company—they are often ready and willing to jump at the next attractive offer. The modern-day mindset is geared toward flexibility and change, not stability and loyalty.

Organizations, meanwhile, often view their employees as little more than resources to be hired, fired, and manipulated as the need arises. The recent recession has only increased the trend toward short-term, bottom-line thinking.

It's gotten so bad that when an employee recently told a CEO that he'd worked for his company for three decades, the

CEO didn't thank him for his loyalty. Instead, his response was, "Why would you stay with a company for 30 years?"[1]

Both sides pay a price for this lack of loyalty. Workers are naturally less happy on the job when they sense little or no loyalty from their employer. They are also less productive. A recent survey found that 74 percent of workers who had survived a company layoff said their productivity had dropped; 64 percent said that coworker productivity had also declined.[2]

According to Timothy Keiningham, author of *Why Loyalty Matters*, less than 30 percent of today's U.S. employees say they are loyal to their companies.

"When you're not loyal to your employer, you're more just like a hostage," Keiningham says. "Employees who are not loyal are thinking about when they can leave. They're not improving their productivity. They're not giving an employer their best, most innovative ideas—because when they leave, they plan on taking those ideas with them."[3]

The effects of organizational disloyalty are alarming:

➤→ People expect to be continually under threat of layoff, so they keep their résumés permanently on the market, changing jobs without concern for anything save their own short-term advantage.

➤→ Because they see executives cheerfully raiding the corporate coffers to enrich themselves, any natural unwillingness to engage in cheating or manipulating the rules to put extra money in their own pockets is lessened.

➤→ When those at the top are obviously interested only in quick, short-term returns (especially for themselves), the attitude permeates the organization as a whole, leading to workers focusing on what will give them the biggest, quickest return—even if that means elbowing colleagues out of the way, playing the dirtier kinds of organizational politics, or hyping résumés to leverage a quick move somewhere else that is paying a few bucks more.

⟫→ Because they recognize that their bosses are on the make and will sacrifice them to hit next quarter's numbers, employees gradually lose the sense that they have an obligation of loyalty to the business. They may still feel loyal to colleagues, but that can turn into an us-versus-them attitude toward those higher up. If people no longer feel that the organization is anything but a short-term meal ticket, they won't invest much of themselves in their job.

⟫→ Worst of all, people start to feel devalued and see their work as less and less worthwhile. This can breed a slew of emotional and psychological stresses and problems.[4]

Lack of loyalty between employers and employees is a serious problem today. What is an aspiring leader to do?

Loyalty at the Bottom of the World

A century ago, a man named Ernest Shackleton was one of the most renowned explorers of his time. He was a member of Captain Randolph Scott's Discovery Expedition to the

Antarctic in 1901–1904 and led the Nimrod Expedition to the Antarctic in 1907–1909, when he and three companions marched farther south than any human had ventured before. He was knighted by the king of England for that effort.

Today, however, Shackleton is best known for a failed mission, the Imperial Trans-Antarctic Expedition of 1914–1917 that aimed to be the first to journey across the southern continent. In January 1915, Shackleton and his men aboard the Endurance were trapped in pack ice in the Weddell Sea and were forced to abandon ship. Under increasingly desperate circumstances, they floated on icebergs and in three small lifeboats to reach a remote, deserted island. From there, Shackleton and five men embarked in one of the lifeboats on an 800-mile voyage through some of the planet's stormiest waters, landing more than two weeks later at South Georgia Island in the South Atlantic. After a rest, Shackleton and two of his men hiked and climbed across the treacherous South Georgia mountains to a whaling station, where Shackleton procured a ship and sailed to rescue his comrades. Despite incredible danger and adversity, every member of the 28-man crew returned home safely.

During all his journeys and particularly on the Endurance Expedition, Shackleton earned the lasting respect and loyalty of his men. Part of the reason was his dedication to their physical health and safety. When the ship was trapped in the pack ice, Shackleton ordered extended times of exercise and games on the ice. Though they were well-stocked with canned foods, he insisted that his men also eat fresh seal meat to prevent scurvy.

Shackleton nurtured his team in other ways. He divided work responsibilities evenly between officers and the rest of the crew and often pitched in himself. He scheduled feasts to mark birthdays and other special occasions and even treated one crewman who suffered from sciatica to two weeks in his cabin.

"He attends to me himself," the crewman wrote in his journal, "making up the fire and making me a cup of tea during the night if I happen to say that I am thirsty, reading to me and always entertaining me with his wonderful conversation, making me forget my pain by joking with me continually just as if I was a spoiled child. What sacrifices would I not make for such a leader as this."[5]

In 1921, Shackleton again set out for the Antarctic on what turned out to be his final voyage. When he died of a heart attack on South Georgia Island, eight of the eighteen crew members were colleagues from the Endurance Expedition.

The loyalty that Shackleton inspired within his crew did not occur by accident. As the leader of missions where the stakes were often life and death, he understood that a bond of loyalty between himself and his men could make the difference between survival and the ultimate failure. He cultivated it constantly.

"The loyalty of your men is a sacred trust you carry," he wrote. "It is something which must never be betrayed, something you must live up to."[6]

Margot Morrell and Stephanie Capparell, in their book *Shackleton's Way: Leadership Lessons from the Great Antarctic*

Explorer, list eight principles Shackleton applied to forge unity and loyalty among his team. As a leader, Shackleton was ahead of his time. His principles are just as important in today's modern workplace as they were in the Antarctic a hundred years ago:

➤➤ Take the time to observe before acting, especially if you are new to the scene. All changes should be aimed at improvements. Don't make changes just for the sake of leaving your mark.

➤➤ Always keep the door open to your staff members, and be generous with information that affects them. Well-informed employees are more eager and better prepared to participate.

➤➤ Establish order and routine on the job so all workers know where they stand and what is expected of them. The discipline makes the staff feel they're in capable hands.

➤➤ Break down traditional hierarchies and cliques by training workers to do a number of jobs, from the menial to the challenging.

➤➤ Where possible, have employees work together on certain tasks. It builds trust, respect, and even friendship.

➤➤ Be fair and impartial in meting out compensations, workloads, and punishments. Imbalances make everyone feel uncomfortable, even the favored.

➤➤ Lead by example. Chip in sometimes to help with the work you're having others do. It gives you the opportu-

➤➤ nity to set a high standard and shows your respect for the job.

➤➤ Have regular gatherings to build esprit de corps. These could be informal lunches that allow workers to speak freely outside the office. Or they could be special holiday or anniversary celebrations that let employees relate to each other as people rather than only as colleagues.[7]

Do you, like Shackleton, constantly cultivate loyalty? If so, you may inspire the kind of loyalty that carries everyone through a crisis—and which leads to lasting success.

The Need to Be Connected

Many companies rely on financial incentives to "buy" loyalty from their employees. They pay higher salaries than the competition or offer deferred compensation such as stock options and generous pensions. And, yes, these do provide a strong reason to stick around in a job, especially during and after a recession. But most people, believe it or not, find little inspiration in the almighty dollar. They may appreciate their salary and show up for work each day yet still lack the motivation they need to do their best.

James Harter of the Gallup research organization says that employee loyalty is based on a number of factors, including whether the employer "looks out for employees' best interests, pays attention to their career path, gives them opportunities to improve their well-being and so forth." Harter, referring to a survey done several years ago that analyzed the reasons people stay with or leave an organization, says that managers play a crucial role in this equation.

"If you're looking for a silver bullet," Harter says, "it is the quality of the relationship between an employee and his or her manager that determines the overall level of employee engagement. Good companies develop a growing list of great managers over time. . . .It's local level teams and how they are connected together by leaders and managers" that have the most impact.

Human nature, Harter adds, "doesn't change when the economy changes. It might take on a different dynamic" during a recession, but what remains constant is "the need to be connected—to a manager, a coworker and/or a purpose, and also the need to be recognized." People's perceptions of their own standards of living "did drop as the economy dropped," he says. But that same drop was not registered in workplaces where employees said they have "someone who encourages their development. There is something about having a mentor, or someone in your life who helps you see the future in the midst of chaos, that can make a difference."[8]

Deborah Small, marketing professor at the Wharton School of the University of Pennsylvania, cites a body of research on what is called "procedural fairness." Procedural fairness suggests that much of what employees feel about an organization "is not the outcomes they get, but the processes. If people feel like processes are handled fairly in the organization, even if they don't get the best for themselves," they tend to be more loyal.

Research also shows that not all behavior is based on self-interest. "Sometimes," Small says, "people do things at considerable cost to themselves, like sticking to a job with lower pay when they could move on and potentially earn more money. It's because we care a lot about relationships and the welfare of others. When we have a relationship with our firm or colleagues, there is a social cost to leaving."

As the leader of your team, it's up to you to establish these kinds of connections with your team in order to inspire loyalty. We've all had a boss who keeps his door shut most of the day, only appearing to point out someone's mistake. You don't want to be that guy. Instead, commit to cultivating a professional yet personal relationship with each person on your team.

Stacey Thomson, public relations manager at the Disney Institute, offers the following tips for fostering positive manager/employee relationships:

➤➤ **Make one-on-one time a priority.** Disney leaders set some time aside each week to sit with cast members one on one. There's usually a business agenda, but the time is really about the relationship. Giving employees an opportunity to just talk about their lives or anything that's frustrating them can do wonders for job performance.

➤➤ **Empower employees to make decisions.** Employees often have the best ideas for improving customer service because they talk to customers all day long. Empower them to make some decisions on behalf of customers. The employee will feel like a contributor, and the customer will be happy that an issue was resolved quickly.

➤➤ **Make yourself available, but don't hover.** Be there to answer questions or help when needed, but give employees the space they need to do their jobs.[9]

When your staff members begin to see you not just as their boss but also more as a mentor or even friend, you are—like Ernest Shackleton—breaking down the barriers that prevent loyalty.

You will also inspire loyalty, of course, when you first demonstrate that same commitment to your company and your team. Auto executive Lee Iacocca accomplished this at a time when the firm he had just joined, Chrysler, was in dire financial straits. In 1978, Iacocca pushed the United Auto Workers to accept salary and benefit cuts, never a popular suggestion. But Iacocca led by example, reducing his own salary to $1 a year.

The gesture impressed Chrysler employees, helping Iacocca win needed concessions from the union. Within five years, the company was restored to financial health.

Employees of Southeastern Freight Lines, a trucking firm, were equally impressed during the recent recession. The company had made a profit each year for more than 50 years, but like everyone else, faced hard choices when the economy contracted. Southeastern's owners and leaders decided that people came before profits. They established a plan to avoid layoffs, even though it might lead to financial losses for a period of time. If they had decided to institute a

5 percent pay cut and stopped the 401k match as many of their competitors had done, they could have come up with over $22 million. They would have ended 2009 in the black. But loyalty to the workers and their well-being was more important to the owners than the company's bank account.

I talked to a Southeastern employee after the plan was announced. He said that the appreciation among workers within the company was unbelievable. Today, attitude and morale at the company are at an all-time high.

Strong leadership inspires strong loyalty.

There's one more way to inspire loyalty among your team members—a method that might surprise you: Lead with humility. Most managers don't think of humility as a key to strong leadership. They figure that they need to appear forceful, confident, and in charge. Humility, they believe, would be viewed as a sign of weakness.

Actually, the opposite is true. It takes confidence and strength to put the interests of others ahead of yourself.

One way to show humility is to give credit to others for your team's successes and take responsibility for your team's failures. Your team is watching you every minute. How you handle these issues will go a long way toward determining the level of loyalty you'll receive from your staff.

I'm reminded of a story about a head basketball coach who called a timeout in the final seconds of the fourth quarter to set up a game-winning play. His assistant coach came up with a strategy the head coach felt would work. The decision was made to go with the assistant's suggestion. When the team in-bounded the ball, however, the play completely backfired, and the game was lost. After the game, a group of disgruntled fans asked, "Who was responsible for that last play?" With his assistant at his side, the head coach answered, "Me." In that moment the head coach gained the loyalty and respect of not only his assistant but also the players.[10]

James Allen, a nineteenth-century writer, said, "You do not attract what you wish, you attract what you are." If you demonstrate a strong measure of loyalty to your team, you'll find that same measure of loyalty being returned to you. By inspiring loyalty, you will lay the foundation for lasting success.

Insights for Inspiration—and Results

▶→ Today, loyalty is lacking among both employees and employers—and both sides pay a price for this.

▶→ The great explorer Ernest Shackleton earned unflinching loyalty from his crews by cultivating it constantly. He considered loyalty a "sacred trust . . . which must never be betrayed."

▶→ The better your connection and relationship with your team, the greater your chances of inspiring loyalty.

▶→ One of the most effective ways to increase employee morale is to demonstrate loyalty.

▶→ The greater the measure of loyalty you show to your people, the more they will respond with the same loyalty toward you.

CARING, PART I

The Physical
Environment

*Too often we underestimate
the power of a touch, a
smile, a kind word, a
listening ear, an honest
compliment, or the smallest
act of caring, all of which
have the potential to turn a
life around.*

Leo Buscaglia

The Physical

D r. Felice Leonardo Buscaglia, who died on June 11, 1998, was a professor in the department of special education at the University of Southern California. Though he was a published author, he would probably have remained unknown in all but academic circles had it not been for one pivotal event—the suicide of one of the university's students deeply moved the professor. Unable to understand what had driven one so young and full of potential to an act so desperate and irrevocable, Buscaglia began to realize how disconnected we are from one another and how valuable simple acts of loving kindness can be.

The professor came to profoundly believe that social bonds are essential, transcending the stresses of everyday life, enriching life above the limitations of poverty, and bridging the communication gaps between generations. He began to teach a noncredit course he called "Love 1A," and thousands of students came to learn.

Buscaglia also began to write books about the essential act of giving and receiving kindness. His works teach us how to deal with death and how to love. In fact, he was so appalled by the lack of literature on this most basic of subjects that he often said, "I got the copyright for love!"

He also apparently had the knack of communicating his ideas because his books were regular entries on the *New York Times* bestsellers list. They were translated into 17 languages and have, to date, sold well over 18 million copies.

What puzzled the professor is that most of us find loving others so embarrassing. Our reticence toward one another at home, in the workplace, and throughout our lives leaves each of us to function in a vacuum of isolation, unable to reach out to others or feel their connection to us.

Buscaglia argued that we must all learn the value of personal attention and learn to overcome the social and mental barriers that inhibit the expression of love and relationship between people, from family to acquaintances, the disabled, the institutionalized, the elderly, and complete strangers. He was passionate about the subject and often made fun of his obsession. He did not apologize for it, however, and he struck a chord with a public that all too often felt detached and alone.

What does this mean for those of us who are trying to become better leaders in the workplace? Do we have to tell our employees that we love them? Must we line them up and hug them at the start of each day?

No, that's probably going a bit too far—you don't want to scare away your staff! It *is* vital, however, that we create a supportive environment if we expect our people to follow our lead and perform at their best. To make this happen, we need to focus primarily on two areas—the physical environment at our office or factory and the social environment that permeates our place of work.

We must establish what I call a culture of caring.

Let's Do This

Warren G. Bennis revolutionized leadership techniques in U.S. industry. He was the U.S. Army's youngest infantry officer in the European theater of operations during World War II, and he was awarded the Purple Heart and Bronze Star.

Management expert Tom Peters has written of Bennis, "His work at MIT in the 1960s, on group behavior, foreshadowed and helped bring about today's headlong plunge into less hierarchical, more democratic and adaptive institutions, both private and public."[1]

Bennis was an inspired innovator who took his vision to institutes of higher learning, such as Cincinnati University and Harvard's John F. Kennedy School of Government Center for Public Leadership. He challenged the prevailing wisdom by showing that leaders with a personal approach who are willing to share authority and responsibility are better suited for dealing with the complexity and change that characterize the modern business environment.

Bennis's impact on the fields of leadership and management theory is significant. His career spans many years. The *Wall Street Journal* named him one of the top 10 speakers on management in 1993; *Forbes* magazine referred to him as the "dean of leadership gurus" in 1996. The *Financial Times* referred to Bennis in 2000 as "the professor who established leadership as a respectable academic field."

In an independent Internet study in 2007, Bennis was voted the fourteenth most influential leadership professional by Gurus International. He has spent time as an advisor to four U.S. presidents and several other public figures, and he has consulted for numerous Fortune 500 companies. Bennis has served on the faculties of Harvard and Boston Universities and taught at the Indian Institute of Management in Calcutta.

Still active in his eighties, Bennis is now distinguished professor of business administration at the University of Southern California. At the same time, he serves as chairman of the advisory board of the Center for Public Leadership at Harvard University's Kennedy School. He is a visiting professor of leadership at the University of Exeter, in England, and a senior fellow at UCLA's School of Public Policy and Social Research.

Makes you tired just thinking about it, doesn't it?

So here we have a man who changed leadership techniques and revolutionized industry. This is what he says about leadership: "Good leaders make people feel that they're at the very heart of things, not at the periphery.

Everyone feels that he or she makes a difference to the success of the organization. When that happens, people feel centered, and that gives their work meaning."[2]

Let's take a closer look at some of the key words in this statement:

➤➤ The very heart of things

➤➤ Makes a difference

➤➤ Centered

➤➤ Meaning

We could phrase this another way: A strong leader brings his or her staff members to the very heart of a project and centers them, letting them know that they make a difference and that their contribution is meaningful and essential. Leaders show them that they care about what staff members do and who they are.

That's being not just a boss, but a leader. What's the difference? We can put it very simply. A boss says, "Do that." A leader says, "Let's do this."

How do you create this sense of a caring community with you at its center rather than at the peak of a pyramid? One major step is providing the right environment.

Know Your Team

I see providing the right environment as a two-tiered plan.

I want you to think about your team members. Right now. Think about each one of them. See their faces. Hear their voices. Could you give me at least one *non-work-related* fact about each one of them? Are they married? Are they parents? Are they happy?

It's important. You need to get to know your team. We have talked about finding a task that suits each one of them. You can't do that unless you know them. Is Bill easily bored? Does he need a constant challenge? Does Elizabeth work best alone, reporting to the group only when her assignment is done? Does John become depressed if he is deprived of light?

Getting to know your team doesn't mean that you have to immerse yourself in their lives, probing their personal business. It doesn't mean that you have to be overly familiar and lose that separation that a leader must sometimes have. It means that you will know them well enough to use them to your best advantage and theirs—starting with creating a physical work space that inspires and leads to results.

First, listen. Do it when your employees are addressing you and when they are engaged in casual conversation. There's no need to eavesdrop. Just pay attention to what goes on around you. If John remarks that January gets to him because it's so gloomy, you might bear that in mind the next time office space near a window is vacant. John might work better and more effectively there.

If Elizabeth often asks everyone to be quieter because she is trying to concentrate, you might move her to a more private corner and keep her need for solitude in mind when you are allotting tasks. As for Bill, don't let him get bored. He will relish the toughest problems and could probably solve them in the midst of a Christmas Eve shopping crowd.

Is Joan always shivering under that heavy jacket she keeps on the back of her chair, while Bob works in his short sleeves, with a damp, red face? They may have different degrees of temperature sensitivity, and the solution may be as simple as switching their desks, moving Bob closer to the air vent and Joan farther from it.

One more thing. If Elizabeth's desk is a model of neatness and Bill prefers working chaos, try not to seat them next to each other. They will drive each other nuts!

Similarly, once Elizabeth is in an environment that allows her to work to her full potential, let her tackle something she has never tried before. Both of you might be surprised at the results.

Make sure that everyone is comfortable. Attention to specific environments will maximize your team's input.

General Environment

We've taken care of the first part of the plan. Next comes the general environment.

Arrive early one morning or stay late one night. Take a good look at the overall working space when it is empty. Ask yourself questions: What does the appearance communicate to the public? Is it attractive and welcoming? Are the colors pleasing? Is it neat and orderly, conveying competence and professionalism? Is there some greenery to add warmth to the atmosphere?

Most managers pay attention to the impression their public areas make on potential customers. They know that the physical environment sends a message. They want their customers to sense that this is a business that values and cares about its clients.

But what about the impression the physical environment makes on your employees? The truth is that the construction and layout of your work space should get across the idea that you value and care about the people working for you. Your team members will get the impression that you promote a double standard if you treat your customers better than you treat them.

Establishing a pleasing physical environment for your employees is simply good business. In 1983, Lockheed Missiles and Space Company (now Lockheed Martin) moved 2,700 engineers and support staff from an old office structure into a new facility, Building 157. Despite the mundane title, the space itself was actually quite innovative. Five stories and nearly 600,000 square feet, it featured a large central atrium, tall exterior windows, light shelves, and sloped ceilings. By incorporating passive solar daylight into the design of Building 157, Lockheed saved half a million dollars in energy bills in the facility's first year of operation.

Building 157's energy savings were overshadowed, however, by an unexpected 15 percent increase in employee productivity and a decrease in absenteeism. Lockheed officials attributed this reinvigoration of their workforce to the design of the building as well. The focus on solar lighting not only reduced energy costs but also helped create a pleasant, productive working environment.[3]

Maybe your company won't authorize an entirely new building. That's okay—there's still plenty you can do to ensure that your team is working in an encouraging space. Below are practical steps you can take to improve the atmosphere and physical conditions for your staff and ultimately the quality of their work:

➤➤ **Ergonomically correct chair:** I love a good chair. Make sure that chairs are comfortable and have adjustable height and arms. When your people sit straight with feet flat on the floor, their arms should be at a 90-degree angle when keyboarding on the computer. If they are having to strain or stretch to reach the computer, then they are putting stress on the back and shoulder area. Chairs can certainly be expensive but in the long run will cost much less than employees spending time at the chiropractor.

➤➤ **Green plants:** My wife and my mother help me with this. Plants do more than just enhance the beauty of your surroundings. Many actually clean pollutants out of the air as they add oxygen and humidity to the indoor environment. They also fight against the common "high-tech ill, sick building disease."

➤➤ **Lighting:** As many studies and our Lockheed example suggest, natural light increases human productivity and reduces fatigue and stress. By simply replacing your antiquated fluorescent bulbs with full-spectrum tubes, you can instantly enhance your environment and your team's well-being. Full-spectrum lighting emits a natural, balanced spectrum of light that is the closest you can get to sunlight indoors. It brings out true, vibrant colors and can ease eye fatigue, improve people's mood, reduce cortisol (stress hormone) levels, slow aging of the retina, and reduce glare.

⟫→ **Air quality:** I have terrible allergies, and good air quality helps me. According to the Environmental Protection Agency, six out of ten buildings are "sick," and indoor air quality is the number one environmental health problem in the United States. A recent study by the U.S. Department of Agriculture found that ionizing a room led to 52 percent less dust and 95 percent less bacteria in the air, since many pollutants found in the air reside on floating dust particles. Check to make sure that heat and air-conditioning units at your facility are functioning properly. When possible, encourage people to open windows to keep fresh air moving through the work space.

⟫→ **Colors:** When I was in grad school, I used to paint to bring in some income, and I learned some interesting things from that experience. Color therapy has its roots in ancient Egypt. Scientific studies recognize that colors bring about emotional reactions in individuals. A simple accent wall can really help an office look more professional and welcoming. Color is so much a part of our lives that we tend to take it for granted. Some companies use colors that they believe will ignite production, like orange (stimulates creativity), yellow (intensifies the intellect and heightens motivation), red (energizes), blue (calming, fights physical and mental tension), and green (fights irritability). As you get to know your team members and their personalities, you may decide that a new paint job may be just the change one or more of them need to boost productivity.

➤➤ **Music:** A large number of offices have some type of music playing in the background. Music can affect emotional well-being, physical health, social functioning, communication skills, and cognitive skills. Music in the workplace, either from piped-in music or from a radio, is sometimes used to mask sounds. Music can provide people with mental stimulation while they are performing monotonous tasks. This can help to reduce stress levels in the office. (I know it works for me and my team when we are stuffing envelopes, filling book orders, or taking inventory.) Some people, however, find music in the office intensely annoying, especially if it is too loud or inappropriate. Find out what's most effective for your team and allow for different methods and tastes when possible.

➤➤ **Breaks:** Even the most focused person needs a break at least twice a day. A change of scenery also helps with emotions. One of the best ways to eliminate stress and recharge the body is to go outside for a 10-minute walk. Encourage your colleagues to focus on their surroundings and take deep breaths. Grab a snack! This will give them renewed energy and will also aid in vitamin D production. Walking will also get the blood and the lymphatic system flowing.

⟫→ **Organization:** An organized environment promotes comfortable, clear thinking. Keep common areas clean and organized. Set an example for your team by making sure your desk is clean and that everything is put away before you leave each day.[4]

Are you starting to see the possibilities? Take another look at your workplace, this time with your employees in mind. Is there enough light, both for all-purpose needs and for specific tasks? Does everyone have enough desk space and a comfortable chair? There is so much you can do. Hang pictures in an empty space. Use charts and plans for current projects to cover blank walls. Have materials enlarged at a print shop if you must. Move a few lamps until the lighting is even and not distracting. Bring in a few plants. Give someone who needs more space an extra desk.

When you've finished with your general impression of the area, move around and look at each staff member's personal space. There is one indicator here that I find most telling: Is that space personalized? If employees add items to a work area that make it particularly theirs, then they feel at home in their environment and are more likely to excel. I would rather find Bill's space cluttered with family photos, pictures drawn by his kids in crayon, and an old sweatshirt with his high school football number on it than find it bare.

A bare space is meant for working. A space Bill thinks of as his own is a place for invention and innovation.

There's an innovator on every team, and everyone can learn from him or her. Make sure that you provide the environment where this can happen. If Bill has a new way to tackle an old task, it may inspire someone else, and that someone could be you. Then other team members will make contributions, and everyone will learn.

The Green Factor

There is one more question to ask as you evaluate the appeal of your work space: How "green" is our business?

A recent poll by MonsterTRAK.com reported that 92 percent of young professionals would rather work for organizations that are environmentally friendly, and 80 percent are interested in securing a job that impacts the environment in a positive way.[5] Members of generation Y prefer to work in a job that supports or promotes what is beneficial to the environment. It might be preventing pollution, reducing the consumption of natural resources, or actively promoting the appreciation of or protection of natural resources.

Even if your business does not do any of these things overtly, you are more likely to attract and retain today's young professional—as well as the mature, environmentally conscious employee—by maintaining a work space that is ecologically friendly. Some choices are obvious: recycle cans, bottles, paper, newspapers, and magazines; find ways to reduce the use of printer paper, such as printing on both sides of a sheet for internal documents; send extra food from company events home with employees or deliver the food to a local charity rather than throw it away. (If you send the food to a charity, make sure your employees know it!)

Another idea is to form a "green team" that can brainstorm and develop ideas for further savings and physical improvements. It's a great way to interact with your employees and allow them to play a role in creating an environment that works for everyone.

The concept, again, is to get to know your people and their values, and respond accordingly. If you demonstrate that you care about their physical environment, it says that you care about them.

But changing your physical work space is only half of the equation for establishing a culture of caring. In the next chapter we look at the second half—the social environment.

Insights for Inspiration—and Results

⇒→ Strong leaders show their employees that they care about them and what they do.

⇒→ Inspiring leaders know their staff well enough to establish a working environment that best suits their needs and personalities.

⇒→ Leaders should demonstrate that they care about their team by maintaining an attractive and comfortable physical environment.

⇒→ Remember that generation me prefers "green" organizations. Do as much as you can to be environmentally friendly.

What Inspires People? 6

CARING, PART II

The Social Environment

> *Take time to appreciate employees and they will reciprocate in a thousand ways.*   Bob Nelson

The Social

Bodily comfort is helpful, but *mental* comfort is paramount. Gripes and little annoyances distract your team and detract from productivity. You, as the leader, are more in charge of this than anyone. You must make sure that the social environment at your workplace reflects a culture of caring.

Most of our workforce feels misunderstood, undervalued, and unappreciated. They want to be a part of something significant. How they are treated can mean much more to them than what they are paid. And when they feel ignored or slighted, it affects their work in negative ways.

Why might your team members feel this way? From my research and what I've heard in conversations with people across the country, here are the main reasons why U.S. workers say they are dissatisfied with their jobs:

➤➤ We're treated like children; we aren't respected.

➤➤ We don't receive what we really need to do the job.

➤➤ We feel unappreciated.

➤➤ We do not enjoy what we do or the people we work with.

As if this list isn't bad enough, here are the reasons why those same workers *hate*—and that's the word they use—their bosses:

➤➤ I know how to do my job; why can't they just let me do it?

➤➤ There are different rules for different people.

➤➤ Management doesn't listen to us.

➤➤ My boss is a terrible manager.

➤➤ There is too much red tape here.

➤➤ Why don't they get rid of all the deadwood around here?

➤➤ There are too many meetings.

➤➤ It's impossible to get promoted here.

➤➤ I hate coming in to work. It's become just a job for me now.

➤➤ My company isn't committed to me, so why should I be committed to it?

Did you feel any of those things before you landed in your current position? Yes you did, and so did the rest of us.

Obviously, no one wants to be hated.

So stop being a boss. Be a leader.

Feeling Good About Where You Work

Leaders find ways to show that they value their employees. It creates a positive working environment, and productivity goes up. Everyone wins.

It helps if the leadership of your company gets this concept. Daimler-Benz, the auto manufacturer, was ahead of the curve in the early 1990s. At its corporate headquarters in Stuttgart, Germany, interior spaces were designed for comfort and efficiency; the employee child-care center was state of the art; a fully equipped fitness center with personal trainers was available to employees during working hours; the cafeteria offered inexpensive, healthy menus; and employees were encouraged to take regular walks on the beautifully landscaped campus.

Daimler senior managers didn't implement these features just because of their good hearts. They believed that a commitment to a positive work environment led to improved attendance and more positive feedback, loyalty, and longevity with the company.[1]

Since then, many other companies have caught on and implemented their own programs to create a more attractive work environment. They've realized that when employees feel good about where they work, they are more productive, innovative, and successful. It just makes sense.

But what can you do on your own to improve the environment for your team? We've already talked about some of it. Talk to your staff members. Listen to them. Ask for their input on what would make them less distracted and more successful on the job.

Stress is an energy-sapper for everyone. You can't expect to eliminate it completely from the workplace, but there are measures you can take to reduce it. For me, running is a great way to decrease stress. My family has a history of heart attacks, so I've been pounding the pavement for more than 20 years. I've found that it does more than just improve my physical health. It's a chance to get away from everything and let my mind wander. I think, plan, strategize, and dream better when I'm alone and running. Some of my best ideas (and I do have a good one every now and then) come when I'm sweaty and pumping my legs.

Not everyone is a runner. You may, however, be able to help your team find other ways to reduce stress. Could you schedule regular walks during the workday? Could you allow someone on your team to take a long lunch break and make up the time later so she can swim at the local pool? Use your imagination. You may be surprised at how effective a creative approach can be.

It's time to center your team. Think in terms of a bicycle wheel. You are the hub, and your team members make up the spokes. Each one radiates from you, yet each is independent and far-reaching. Each is an essential part of the whole, joined by and supporting the rim and the tire. Without the hub, the spokes will fall apart and be useless, and the hub has no purpose without the spokes.

The rim is a project. Once the tire is in place, the project is complete.

When the wheel is put into motion, the hub turns first, spinning on the axle that is the corporation. The hub turns the spokes, but only if they are firmly attached to it. Yet the point at which the spoke attaches to the hub is only a very small percentage of its whole. Without that point, it cannot function, but the main part of its capability reaches far from the center.

Your job is to keep each team spoke attached to you and, through you, to its partners, while allowing room for it to fully perform its allotted and essential task.

The hole can be drilled, the spoke can be inserted, but the weld provides the environment that keeps everything together. You are the weld—the strength of the joint. You are the proper environment.

Once you think of your team in this way, each element depending on the other and all of them depending on you, you will see the value of caring for each spoke so clearly that doing it will become second nature.

Respect will be inevitable, in both directions. Each element will have a sense of total commitment to the others, and feel it from them. There will be a cooperative working environment. Each member of the team will be strongly centered, firmly rooted in the hub, and free to reach out from it. The wheel will turn.

Now let's apply a little oil.

Say Something Nice

George and Mary Lou were celebrating their golden wedding anniversary. A reporter, noting that so many marriages end in divorce, wondered what secret had enabled them to keep their relationship strong for 50 years. "What is your recipe," the reporter asked George, "for a long, happy marriage?"

George answered that just after his wedding, his new father-in-law pulled him aside and gave him a gift. It was a gold watch, one that George still wore all these years later. He drew up his sleeve to show the reporter. Imprinted on the face of the watch were the words George had read several times each day for the last five decades: "Say something nice to Mary Lou."[2]

A simple reminder of our appreciation for someone else—especially when it's sincere and repeated often—can be incredibly powerful. It can be the glue that holds a marriage together. It also can be the spark that inspires a team of employees to reach for new levels of success.

I experienced this power myself. During my high school summers, I worked for a place called Oxen Hill Rentals. It rented out every kind of machine tool known to humanity—lawnmowers, bulldozers, chainsaws, and more. My job in the warehouse was to keep the equipment cleaned, gassed up, and oiled for the next customer. The worst job was cleaning the five-foot-long sewer coils used to drain raw sewage from an industrial site. These might come back 50 at a time, covered with slime. Sometimes I couldn't find my gloves and ended up cleaning these things with my bare hands. It was hard, fast, and nasty work. If a tool wasn't ready when a customer wanted it, my boss noticed, and I heard about it.

When we worked hard and had a good week at Oxen Hill Rentals, however, our bosses noticed that too. They sometimes showed their appreciation by adding a little bonus to our paychecks. At other times, they ordered seafood and pizza at the end of the day on Fridays for the crew to enjoy. We definitely worked up an appetite on that job, so heaping plates of food made a lasting impression.

Those small touches created a highly positive attitude at OHR. Despite the difficult work, I enjoyed being there. I felt like more than just a lowly high school kid helping the company make money. I believed my bosses noticed and valued my efforts. That motivated me to keep doing my best.

In your role as leader, it's a great idea (when it's deserved) to give a team member who has not asked for one a raise or bonus. The other staff members will likely try just a little bit harder if they know the same might happen to them.

Most baby boomers understand this approach. For them, a steady paycheck was what counted. It motivated them to do their best. While helpful, however, money is no longer the primary inspiration for many of today's employees. Instead, they're looking just as much for positive reinforcement and relationships.

A recent survey of modern employees supports this idea. Number three on the list of motivating factors is "assistance with personal problems." Number two on the list is a feeling that they are "in on things." And the number one motivator for employees is "full appreciation for work done."[3]

These are not expensive, time-consuming measures to implement. It doesn't take that much effort to check in with your team members and find out how they're doing on a personal level. If they're dealing with a sick child or other difficult situation at home, your willingness to temporarily allow them a flexible schedule can make all the difference to them. Simply by asking the question and listening, you may help them get through a hard time—and help them perform better while they're at the office.

It's also not that tough to keep your team up to date on what's happening on your project and with the rest of the organization. Through meetings, messages, and conversations, make sure you give your employees *more* than what they need to accomplish their tasks. Sharing information shows that you trust and value your team.

As for that top motivator—appreciation for work accomplished—you'd better make it a priority if you want to be an effective leader. Failure to acknowledge good work is one of the quickest ways to lose your best people.

This is just what happened recently at a school. Peter was the school janitor. He also happened to be one of the school's most well-liked employees—at least by the kids. Peter always greeted the children with a smile, asked how their day was going, and was ready to lend a hand if they needed help. One student said she knew he was happy with his job "because he was always smiling and spoke kindly with everyone. You could just tell he enjoyed being a part of our school."

Peter was one of the unique individuals at the school who made it a positive experience for its "customers," the students. Too bad school administrators never took the time to notice. Instead, they took advantage.

Over a period of months, the school's leadership team assigned Peter more and more tasks that they expected to be completed before the children arrived at school. Peter realized that this workload was becoming increasingly unfeasible, so he went to see the school's administrator to discuss the situation. Peter pointed out that even though he arrived at school every morning at 6 a.m., he still didn't have enough time to complete all the tasks that were being assigned to him.

The administrator responded by telling Peter he'd just have to come to the school an hour earlier so that the work would be completed before the children arrived. Given this perfunctory and rather dismissive reaction, Peter realized that the school's administration wasn't interested in working with him to find a more reasonable solution. Reluctantly, he quit his job as the school's custodian.

The children noticed immediately. Peter was no longer in the hallway to greet and encourage them. They valued him and now missed him. School was no longer quite as positive, enjoyable, or inspiring. Perhaps because school administrators viewed Peter as a lowly staff member, they failed to appreciate his contributions. Their lack of understanding cost them a valuable member of the team and moved them further away from their goal of offering an excellent educational experience.[4]

Demonstrating appreciation is important. Your team won't reach its full potential without it.

This is especially true of the modern employee. In fact, today's younger workers don't just *want* appreciation. They *need* it. Tony Zinni, coauthor of *Leading the Charge: Leadership Lessons from the Battlefield to the Boardroom*, says that a recent survey of employees by the manager of the recruiting division for a major corporation showed a big difference in the expectations of baby boomers and younger workers:

> Older employees tended to see rewards in the form of increases in pay, while younger employees wanted rewards in the form of greater public recognition of their accomplishments—nonmonetary awards such as certificates, plaques, and trophies; they preferred these to larger paychecks. To hear "I'm proud of you" with a handshake from the boss and a photo with him or her is more powerful for them than an impersonal material benefit, especially if the recognition is public, documented, and well deserved.
>
> This new form of recognition came very close to me when my own daughter, Maria, made it clear that I had to be present when she received an achievement award at Vanguard (the mutual fund company) from the then CEO, John Bogle, the legendary founder of the Vanguard Group. The event took place in Bogle's office. During a long chat afterward when he personally expressed his appreciation for her work, her pride and satisfaction were clearly evident. A pay raise alone or some impersonal ceremony would not have had the same effect. As a proud father, I could see how much the personal touch meant to her.[5]

Appreciating Your Team

How can you as a leader show appreciation for your team and create a culture in which employees do the same for each other? Here are a few suggestions from Bob Adams, author of *The Everything Leadership Book*:

➤→ Create a vehicle for individual employees to recognize other employees who help them in ways that are frequently overlooked—personal recognition for the person who is always there in a pinch.

➤→ Develop a program to recognize teams that work especially well together to achieve a defined objective. Make the guidelines measurable and linked to the business objective.

➤→ Reinvent and consistently follow the employee-of-the-month program that most companies have had in the past. The key is to keep it going and to make the award meaningful. How are employees recognized? How does everyone learn about this? Do all the employees of the month get together at certain times of the year?

➤→ Create employee-of-the-month focus groups where those employees are asked to assist with business problem solving and creative strategic development.

➤→ Periodically surprise everyone with a special award: the "Just Because You Did a Great Job Award." Pretty soon, people will begin doing the kinds of things you appreciate in the hope that they'll receive one of these coveted awards. It's a great way to develop your company culture quickly.

➤➤ Rather than having a discipline procedure that tracks only problems and performance issues, have a performance development policy that offers managers the opportunity to praise employees when they reach a new milestone in personal professional development. No longer will people fear the personnel file; they will want to get statements of positive development put in their file.

➤➤ Don't forget the tried and true five-, ten-, and fifteen-year seniority awards, plaques, and events. Again, the key is consistent application of these procedures, especially when times are not so good and cash flow is low. This is not the time to skimp on these awards. People need to have some sense of security during really slow business times.

➤➤ It may sound simple, but a friendly note to say "thank you" goes a long way. Consider writing notes to people you catch doing something the way you want it done. Again, the key is to make it personal and to consistently follow through.[6]

Some bosses are passionate about discovering mistakes, problems, and people whose performance is below par. You've probably worked for some of them. These shortcomings do need to be addressed, but they must be balanced with a passion for seeking out and celebrating good work.

I once heard someone say that 70 percent of people have never heard the words "thank you" at their place of work. Make sure that the members of your team never say that about your office.

Personal and organizational displays of appreciation may not seem like much, but they can make each and every one of us feel, for just a moment, that the universe centers around us and that we matter. If we feel this, we will feel better about ourselves and we will perform better, trading on a new sense of self-worth.

To continue our wheel metaphor from earlier, you are the hub, your spokes are connected to you, and the wheel is turning. Personal attention is the oil that smooths its progress.

Think. There are many things you can do on a personal level to strengthen your spokes' connection to you, and you can do them without impairing your position as a leader. In fact, they will add to your position as a leader.

Your staff will band together to acknowledge landmark occasions such as birthdays, weddings, births, illness, and death. You can commemorate other events as well. Did someone voluntarily stay late to keep a project on schedule? Bob Adams already recommended leaving a personal note. You can make your appreciation even more memorable by sending flowers or fruit to your team member's home. It will take 10 minutes and cost a few bucks, but that team member will never forget it.

Make a habit of calling or sending an e-mail to any employee who has put in extra effort. Send small gifts, like a gift card to a nice local restaurant for the entire team, once a project or step has been successfully completed.

Why not ambush John at the elevator, shake his hand, and thank him for doing a good job that day? His smile will repay you for the effort, and he will come into work with a new purpose the next morning.

Praise is a key component for creating a positive social environment. But empty praise—telling employees they're "wonderful" or a "genius" even though they haven't done anything special that day—actually takes away from what you are trying to accomplish. They'll wonder, *Does he really mean it?*

Your words will be much more effective if they address a specific achievement: "Sharon, your presentation was right on target. The statistics you included backed up your point perfectly," or, "Dave, I saw how you took care of that unhappy customer. I appreciate how you listened to him tell the whole story and patiently explained what his options were." That's genuine. It shows you're paying attention to what they do.

It's also important to communicate your appreciation as quickly as possible. For most of their lives, many of today's employees have been heavily praised by parents, teachers, and others for meeting basic benchmarks: showing up on time and finishing a task. They're used to lots of immediate, positive feedback and get nervous if the boss doesn't say anything.

To the majority of the men and women under age 40, no news is bad news. Your quick response to that just-completed project—even if it's not all positive—will wash away fears and keep your team coming back for more.

Leading is not just about results, quality, productivity, and sales. It's also about people. If you spend the majority of your time focused on the "things" of business and forget about your team, you are headed for trouble. Great leaders know they must invest in learning about people, developing people, serving people, encouraging people, and *inspiring* people. It can start by establishing a culture of caring.

The Beatles' song "All You Need Is Love" is a good motto for any leader. Kindness and appreciation—the little things that show you care about your team—add up to big results. They will inspire your group to new heights.

I'm sure Leo Buscaglia would agree: All you need is love.

Insights for Inspiration—and Results

➤➤ For modern employees, how they are treated can be more important than what they are paid.

➤➤ When employees feel good about where they work, they are more productive, innovative, and successful.

➤➤ Today's workers place tremendous importance on being appreciated for their efforts. Whether it's through a bonus, time off, an award, or a thank-you note, show that you appreciate your team.

➤➤ Fast and appropriate feedback is a great way to show your staff members that you notice and care about what they do.

What Inspires People? 7
➤➤ UNDERSTANDING

> *Seek first to understand and then to be understood.*
>
> Stephen Covey

A doctor was having a conversation with the mother of a 16-year-old. The mother said with confidence that she knew her daughter so well that she understood her "from head to toe."

A few minutes later the daughter walked into the room and joined the discussion. The doctor asked the daughter how much, on a scale of one to ten, she felt understood by her mother. The daughter's answer was "six."

The mother immediately got defensive. She verbally attacked her daughter. When the daughter tried to explain why she didn't feel understood, the mother interrupted and debated with her, starting an argument. Finally, in frustration, the mother walked out of the room, leaving the daughter feeling less understood than ever.

Sometimes we don't understand the people around us nearly as well as we think we do. That's often the case with leaders in the workplace. Most employees today do not feel understood by their bosses. We learned in the last chapter that the younger members, especially, of today's workforce have enjoyed immediate and usually positive feedback for most of their lives. They get very uncomfortable when the boss is silent. They feel he or she isn't in tune with them. They wonder about their place in the company. Some become so unsettled that they quickly move on to a new job.

That's why successful leaders in the twenty-first century strive to develop a relationship with their employees. This is exactly what today's employees want.

It's important to remember that most baby boomers grew up in traditional families in a relatively stable society. That's far less likely to be true for generation Xers and Yers. For these men and women, divorce, broken homes, and single-parent households are almost the norm. In many cases, their parents either had to work long hours to make ends meet or their parents became workaholics. It left many of their children feeling hurt, unloved, and misunderstood. The relationship was lacking.

When these young workers begin a new job, they can't help wondering, consciously or unconsciously, if their boss will be like their parents. Will his style be militant and abrasive? Is she interested in her employees as people, or does she care only about the bottom line?

Typically, the modern employee mindset differs greatly from that of previous generations. These young men and women are dedicated to their families and see their job—and their boss—as an extension of that. Work is part of their life but not the center of their life. They desire encouragement, purpose, and connection (just look at Facebook).

They come to work seeking relationships. They want to be understood.

There are definite parallels here to one of the most intimate relationships of all—marriage. Countless divorces have resulted from a misunderstanding of the basic, but different, desires of women and men. A common response in marriage surveys is that women want love, and men want respect.

Several years ago, a young woman went on a retreat about relationships. At the first session, the retreat facilitator divided the room, men on one side, women on the other. "I'm going to ask you to choose between two bad things," he said. "If you had to choose, would you rather feel alone and unloved in the world *or* would you rather feel inadequate and disrespected by everyone?"

What kind of choice is that? the young woman thought. *Who would ever choose to feel unloved?*

The facilitator turned to the guys. "Okay, men," he said. "Who here would rather feel alone and unloved?" A sea of hands went up. Many of the women gasped. Only a few men raised their hands to choose being disrespected.

Then it was the women's turn. The men in the room were equally surprised when most of the women chose feeling disrespected over feeling unloved.[1]

When we fail to understand the most fundamental needs and wants of our partners—or our colleagues—relationships suffer, communication breaks down, and both sides fall short of their potential. Often, the relationship grows so dysfunctional that it can't be repaired.

In the case of a marriage, a wife who enjoys teasing her husband in public, especially in front of other men, likely won't understand why he grows angry and cuts off the conversation. She doesn't realize that what she views as harmless teasing, he sees as embarrassing and blatant disrespect. Likewise, a husband who doesn't remember his wife's birthday or their anniversary will probably hurt her deeply. In her eyes, he's demonstrated that his love for her isn't that strong.

It's important that we understand the basic desires of our employees as well. Being treated with respect might be a fundamental need for Jason. For Joanne, regular feedback on her performance might be the core issue that makes the difference between her feeling uncertain and unmotivated and feeling inspired. Only when we truly understand our team members and their unique personalities, qualities, and desires are we positioned to lead successfully and with confidence.

It Starts at the Top

Peter Drucker, known as the father of modern management, wrote, "The first secret of effectiveness is to understand the people with whom one works and on whom one depends, and to make use of their strengths, their ways of working, and their values. For working relations are as much based on the person as they are based on the work."[2]

It often starts at the top. Norman Mayne, CEO of Dorothy Lane Market, a specialty-food supermarket chain based in Dayton, Ohio, has met with every new hire at the company for over 20 years. The meetings are more than just a moment to shake hands with the boss. Mayne takes time to discuss the company's culture, customers, and competitors. Both sides come away with a better understanding of each other. It's no coincidence that Dorothy Lane is flourishing despite its location near ten Walmart and five Kroeger stores.[3]

No matter where you are in the hierarchy of your company or organization, it makes sense for you to get to know your team members and to try to understand their individual needs and dreams. I don't mean that you have to be buddies with each of them, hanging out together at the links or the mall on weekends. But your willingness to put yourself in their shoes and see the world from their perspective will give you valuable insight into how to bring out their best.

A big part of getting the best from your team members is helping them grow. This has never been more important than it is today. A recently retired executive vice president for operations at the Bank of New York said that an increased emphasis on counseling and mentoring was the biggest change he'd seen in his years in the banking industry.

"Counseling and mentoring are no longer optional," he said. "They're expected and demanded by those we lead."[4]

Many modern firms have established formal, structured programs to identify and develop promising leaders to take those firms into the future. Some companies hire professional coaches to guide these young stars. Retention—"grow your own and keep them"—is valued more than ever before.

But counseling and mentoring don't work if there isn't genuine understanding of the individual. There are no factories that churn out great leaders like trucks on an assembly line. All members of your team have unique characteristics that affect their work and how they fit into your vision for success. It's up to you to discover those distinctive qualities and manage them effectively.

After I received my undergraduate degree at Columbia International University, I went back to school to earn a master's degree in teaching. One of my professors there was as tough as they come. She was always after me to do better. Though she seemed to go easy on other students, I could never satisfy her.

This professor observed one of my final teaching sessions in front of a class. Our follow-up meeting went true to form—she unloaded a long list of issues on me that needed work.

Later, I complained to a classmate about how unhappy my professor was with me. "You're kidding!" my friend said. "She told me that you were really improving, that your last lesson was the best you'd ever done."

That's when the lightbulb went on for me. I realized that my professor knew me better than I did. She understood that I had natural ability as a speaker and that I tended to rely on that when I taught. I was just getting by. She knew I was capable of more and kept after me, trying to motivate me to do my best.

You can motivate and develop the members of your work team in a similar way. Instead of immediately telling your employees the answer when they run into an obstacle, give them time to uncover a solution on their own. It will allow them to stretch their abilities and be better employees—and leaders—down the road.

A few years after my experience with my professor, I discovered how motivation worked from the other side of the desk. I'd had some success as a high school basketball player and was named conference most valuable player in my senior year. I became a basketball coach and spent six years leading a team of teenage boys. I quickly learned about the different personality types on my team and how to tailor my style to each player.

I remember one game in which right from the start my point guard was making sloppy passes and turning the ball over. It wasn't like him at all. Something, either grades or girlfriend problems, was distracting him. I had to get in his face. "C'mon!" I said. "Get focused. We are playing a game here."

That was all he needed. When I aggressively showed my dissatisfaction, he snapped out of it and started playing up to his potential.

My shooting guard, on the other hand, required the opposite treatment. When he played poorly, my yelling only made it worse. Instead, I needed to call him over to the sideline and ask in a gentle voice, "Hey, are you all right? Is something going on? We can talk about it later, but right now I need you to concentrate on the game." That wouldn't have meant anything to my point guard, but for my shooting guard, it was the most effective approach.

As you observe and talk with your team members, ask yourself a few questions about each one. Is she usually quiet or vocal? Is he usually defensive or assertive? When something unexpected happens and you need to encourage them to work hard and fast, will you be more effective with a hand on the shoulder or a kick (figuratively) in the behind?

Don't wait for a crisis to determine the answers. You need to understand the individual characteristics of each member of your team now so you can have a plan ready.

For years, a father named Roger had pushed Gordon, his oldest son, to be a better student. Roger was always a little disappointed in Gordon and his B grades. The son never quite measured up to the father's expectations.

When Gordon was a senior in high school, Roger was puzzled by an invitation to a student awards assembly. He couldn't imagine any awards that Gordon would win. Roger went to the event anyway, but grew increasingly annoyed at watching other students march up the aisle for applause. Why was he here? Why was his son so mediocre? Finally, the principal came to the last presentation— a new award for an exceptional student. Roger was astonished to hear Gordon's name announced, followed by a long description of his son's fine character, kindness, trustworthiness, and quiet leadership. The principal concluded by thanking Gordon and saying, "No one who has really gotten to know you will ever be quite the same again."[5]

Roger was so focused on grades that he didn't really know his son or appreciate the gifts he brought to the people around him. Don't make the mistake Roger made. Learn what makes your people who they are, their strengths and weaknesses, passions and problems, and you'll be in a far better position to inspire them to do their best.

Understanding Poor Performance

It's inevitable that there will be times when you're unhappy with the performance of someone on your staff. In the old days, the answer was often to try to force improvement. "Shape up or ship out" was the motto. The attitude among most leaders was that the employee needed the job more than the company needed the employee. If someone wasn't adjusting well or doing the job, then it was time to move on to someone else.

Today, many leaders realize that there may be more efficient and less expensive ways of getting the results they want than starting over. Once again, it is rooted in trying to understand the employee and the problem at hand.

Tony Zinni elaborates:

> The hire-and-fire mentality has been replaced by a developmental approach. We ask questions today that seek to identify causes for deficiencies in skill or aptitude, or for lack of motivation, poor attitudes, inability to meet objectives, or other factors that create obstacles to performance. Solutions come in the form of training, counseling and mentoring, improvement of work environment, removal of obstacles to performance, incentives, and inclusion in decision making.
>
> Successful enterprises now view training and education programs as critical investments in their people; no longer are they considered luxuries that are the first to go onto the chopping block when budgets get tight.

These programs have exponential payoffs that many old-school leaders have never been able to realize. In addition to increasing productivity, they build loyalty and improve retention.[6]

Knowing your staff's strengths and weaknesses enables you to respond wisely when you are choosing a team for an important project. Remember Shackleton, the intrepid Antarctic explorer? When it was time to choose his companions for the dangerous, all-or-nothing voyage in a lifeboat to South Georgia Island, he had the strengths and weaknesses of his men at the top of his list of considerations.

Navigator Frank Worsley was an obvious pick for the journey; they would never make it without someone skilled at guiding them by the stars. Timothy McCarthy was an experienced seaman and liked by all, a good man to have on a long voyage. In addition, Shackleton chose Tom Crean, also an experienced seaman, tough and tactless; carpenter Harry McNeish, who might be able to repair any damage to the boat; and seaman John Vincent. These last three were chosen for their abilities, but also for their liabilities. Shackleton feared they would damage the morale of the men left behind if they were removed from his influence.[7]

Sometimes, of course, problems are difficult to fix even with training and mentoring. In these cases, you have to decide whether or not the employee has a future with your firm of if you'd all be better served by letting the person go. The more you know and understand the person, the more likely you are to make the right decision.

Wayne Downing was a four-star general with the U.S. Army. He said that, "Most of my bad judgment calls were generally about people. There have been times when I knew I had to take people out of a position. I knew they weren't going to change, and they weren't going to do what had to be done. But it's traumatic when you do that. The higher up you go, the more traumatic it is for the organization to remove people, and you don't like to do that, but in the final analysis you have to."[8]

As a leader, you're bound to make some personnel mistakes over the years. But if you know your team well, you'll have the knowledge you need to make informed decisions, difficult as they may be. If you truly understand your staff, most of the time you'll get it right.

Good Listening

If there is one key to understanding the members of your staff, it probably lies in *listening* to them. We all have ears to hear what people are saying, but much of the time what we hear is forgotten a few minutes later. Good listening is something else entirely. It's taking in what your team member is saying, chewing on it a while, and letting it digest in your system.

Simon Verity is a sculptor and master stone carver who honed his craft restoring thirteenth-century cathedrals in Great Britain. His hands were, of course, critical to his art. You might be surprised to know that his ears were just as important.

With each blow of his chisel, Verity listened carefully to the sounds that echoed off the stone. A solid resonance indicated that all was well. But a higher-pitched *ping* meant that a piece of rock might be ready to break off. Verity constantly adjusted the angle of his blows and the force of his mallet to these pitches, pausing frequently to run his hand over the freshly carved surface. His success depended on his ability to hear and interpret the sounds of the stones.

As leaders, we too need to be active listeners. The words your employees use, combined with their tone and facial expressions, are a window into what's in their hearts. You'll learn a lot by looking for the meaning behind the words, not only about your staff member but also about how to head off small problems before they turn into disasters. The old Cherokee proverb still applies today: "Listen to the whispers, and you won't have to hear the screams."

Sometimes you won't be too happy about what you hear from your staff. It may not reflect well on you. A strong leader, however, never lets negative feedback get in the way of good listening and growth.

I once was asked to evaluate the interactions at a particular company. The boss was a very positive guy, which is a good thing. However, he was so focused on making every conversation upbeat that he sent the unspoken message that no one should ever say a discouraging word. This boss avoided negativity and confrontations at all costs. The problem with this philosophy is that it stops the flow of communication and creativity. Encouraging input from your employees, even when it's negative, can lead to some of the best ideas—and prevent some of the worst.

Red Auerbach was one of the most successful professional basketball coaches of all time, winning nine NBA championships with the Boston Celtics (did I mention that I like basketball?). One reason for his success was that he was a good listener.

Bill Russell, Auerbach's all-star center, has told the story of the day the coach announced to his team he'd designed a new play that would bring them their next title. Auerbach showed the team his play and had them practice it for more than an hour. Then, chest out and hands on his hips, he proudly called the team together.

Russell continues the story with Auerbach addressing the team:

> "Well, Cooz, whaddaya think?"
>
> Cousy shrugged. "I think it's a piece of crap, Red."
>
> There was dead silence in the gym.
>
> Then Red turned to Sharman, who told him the same thing—but a little more politely: "Well, Red, if you go here with this guy and there with that guy, then you've got no one to slide over and cover here. The whole play breaks down, it's just a waste of time."
>
> Now the silence in the place was thick as a blanket.
>
> Red turned to me. "How 'bout you, Russ?"
>
> "Those are the two most articulate guys on the club, Red. I can't say it any better!"
>
> Now Red could have imposed the play on us, insisted we run it because he knew it would really work, but instead we never heard about it again. And he never took it back to the drawing board to rework it that season

or in any season following. Red listened, and when he heard the team unite in their opposition, he didn't fight it. He let it go.[9]

Auerbach had just as big an ego as the next guy, but he was smart enough to follow the advice of his team. He wanted to win more than he wanted to be right about a pet idea. He was willing to listen.

When you talk with your team, it's a good idea to ask open-ended questions. Seek feedback on yourself, on the company and its direction, and on what can improve your employees' work and personal lives. Then *listen* to their answers.

Peter Drucker said, "Organizations are no longer built on force. They are increasingly built on trust. Trust does not mean that people like one another. It means that people can trust one another. And this presupposes that people understand one another."[10]

Once your team members see your efforts to understand them, they'll be encouraged to share more openly with you, giving you the knowledge you need to be an effective and inspiring leader.

Insights for Inspiration—and Results

⟫→ Most of today's employees come to work seeking relationships. They want to be understood.

⟫→ Counseling and mentoring are expected in today's workplace.

➤➤ The better you understand strengths and weaknesses of your staff members, the easier it will be to motivate them and develop their talents.

➤➤ Listening to—and when appropriate, implementing—ideas suggested by your team engenders respect and trust.

What Inspires People?

8

➤➤ PATIENCE

L et's pretend that you are a first-grade elementary school teacher. You have thirty-one kids in your class. It's Monday morning, and it's raining. I mean really raining, coming down in buckets. The time is 8:15 a.m., and here come the buses full of children. You go into the hallway to meet the kids and take off thirty-one pairs of boots and thirty-one raincoats. You put the boots away, hang up the raincoats, and send your students into your classroom. Class begins.

One hour and twenty minutes later it's time for recess. You put on thirty-one pairs of boots and thirty-one raincoats. Twenty minutes later, recess is over. You take off thirty-one pairs of boots and thirty-one raincoats, and class begins again.

One hour and thirty minutes later, it's lunchtime. After eating, you help the children go outside again. You again put on thirty-one pairs of boots and thirty-one raincoats. Twenty minutes later, lunchtime is over, and you take off thirty-one pairs of boots and thirty-one raincoats. It's time for afternoon lessons.

An hour later, it's time for afternoon recess. More pairs of boots. More raincoats.

Finally, the end of the school day arrives. You're exhausted, and your back is killing you. Once again, you help your students into their boots and raincoats. When you get to the thirty-first student, you tug that last boot on and stand up. He looks up at you, and you look down at him. He says, "These aren't my boots."

You don't say a word, but you want to pull your hair out. You are thinking, "Are you kidding me!" So you just bend over and take his boots off. Your back creaks when you stand and look down at him. Then he looks up at you and says, "Those are my brother's boots, but he let me wear 'em today."

At this point, you're ready to scream or to run as fast as you can and never look back, or both. But you don't. You calmly put those boots back on that last little boy and send him on his way.

Most teachers (and parents of young children) must have been given an extra dose of the virtue called *patience*. Without it, sooner or later they'd all end up in straitjackets!

As a leader, you also are going to need an extra dose of patience. Without even meaning to, your staff will test you and push you to your limit. There will be times when it feels as if you spend the entire day helping every member of your team through the same mundane tasks, over and over and over. At other times your staff will do the exact opposite of what you thought you asked for. Staff members will invest significant time and resources in a report on the wrong project. They'll leave your most important client sitting alone in the lobby because two hours ago you asked them to clean the coffeepot.

Your employees are going to make mistakes, and when they do, your ability to respond with patience and understanding will set the tone for every future interaction with your team. Your patience will earn their admiration. It will also be better for your blood pressure.

When Jean misses an important phone appointment because she took a long lunch and you know it will cost your company thousands of dollars, your screaming "What were you thinking?" isn't going to solve the problem. It's a better idea (after counting to 10, if needed) to ask her in an even and nonthreatening tone, "Jean, what happened? Did you forget about the appointment? Did something delay you?" Give her a chance to explain. Even if there isn't a good explanation, deal with the situation in a rational manner. When you lose your temper, you also lose the respect of your team.

Your demonstration of patience will do more than make you appear cool-headed in a crisis. You'll be teaching your team how to be patient themselves. In today's workplace, that lesson is more vital than ever.

Top Secret

When I was in college and needed a summer job to help pay for tuition, I sent an application to a general government pool. A couple of weeks later, I was called in to interview at Bolling Air Force Base in Washington, DC. The woman who interviewed me began asking all kinds of penetrating questions. I learned that an extensive background check had been done on me, all the way back to my elementary school years in Wisconsin. To my amazement (and horror), they'd even talked to my old girlfriends!

Then the woman began complimenting me on my outstanding work record and performance at a high school leadership conference. I put two and two together and figured I was being considered for something big. Jeremy Kingsley was about to serve as a key asset for his country.

Maybe they want me to be the driver for a general, I thought. Or maybe a clerk, handling top-secret documents. Or just maybe they're planning to train me as a spy. They might even have a mission in mind for someone just my age. I might be going undercover!

The interview finished well. Later, I received a call to report to Building P20 at the base at 8 a.m. the following Monday. Not surprisingly, I thought, they didn't reveal my assignment over the phone.

I could hardly stand the anticipation as I waited for Monday. Maybe, like James Bond, I would be introduced to the air force's version of "Q" and outfitted with special weapons, like chewing gum that could be used as a hand grenade.

On Monday, I arrived at 8 sharp. The lettering on the door at Building P20 said "Office of Special Investigations." I could hardly breathe. This was the real thing. OSI is like the FBI for the air force.

Soon I was ushered in to meet a stern-looking sergeant. I was about to discover my future.

The sergeant got right to the point. "Welcome to OSI," he said. "We've been informed that you're going to be our new head of janitorial services."

All my dreams of espionage and dangerous undercover missions disappeared faster than a super villain's speedboat. I wasn't going to be a top-secret agent. I was going to be a top-secret janitor!

Actually, it wasn't so bad. I had access to places that most people only dream of, even though my mission there was only to change light bulbs, vacuum, and take out the trash. I remained at that job for three years, staying on after I graduated.

It *was* a little humiliating when the new air force recruits, seventeen- and eighteen-year-olds fresh out of high school, were bused in and dropped off at the base while I worked outside. Part of my duty was keeping the grounds clean. These guys—I called them "no-stripes"—used to give me a bad time and throw cigarette butts in my direction for me to pick up.

Man, something doesn't seem quite right here, I thought. I'm picking up after these guys, and I'm the one with the college degree.

But I knew I was doing good work and building my résumé. I earned a raise after each year at the base. I realized that even though it wasn't the dream job I originally envisioned, it was a step toward a better future. I just had to be patient. As Arnold Glasgow has said, "The key to everything is patience. You get the chicken by hatching the egg, not smashing it."

I have wondered how many of today's young career climbers would be willing to work as a janitor, even if it was as a top-secret janitor? Many have grown up in an instant-gratification world. They're conditioned to expect meals that are ready in 30 seconds or less, problems on TV that are solved in 60 minutes or less, and immediate communication by cell phone and Internet. The concept of *wait* does not fit in their lifestyle.

A would-be novelist named Kathryn Stockett didn't buy into this desire for instant gratification. She spent a year and a half writing a manuscript, polished it, and mailed it to a literary agent. Six weeks later, she received a rejection letter that said, "Story did not sustain my interest."

Instead of being discouraged, Kathryn was thrilled. She called friends and told them she'd received her first rejection letter. She went back to editing, sure that she could improve her story. Several months later, she sent the revised manuscript to more agents. This time Kathryn received 15 rejections. "Maybe the *next* book will be the one," a friend said. But Kathryn remained patient. She still believed in her original idea.

A year and a half later, Kathryn opened her fortieth rejection, which said, "There is no market for this kind of tiring writing." Another friend's comment was, "You have so much resolve, Kathryn. How do you keep yourself from feeling like this has been a huge waste of time?"

That was a tough weekend for Kathryn. She cried a bit. She didn't bother to get dressed but stayed in her pajamas. But she didn't give up. She resolved to make more improvements to her manuscript and see where it would lead.

The revisions and rejections continued—45, 50, 55. Kathryn even insisted on rewriting the last chapter an hour before she was due at the hospital to give birth to her daughter.

It takes a great deal of persistence and patience to work through 60 rejections of a manuscript. That's where Kathryn Stockett found herself after five years of writing and rewriting. Yet Kathryn's tenacity paid off. The sixty-first letter was from an agent named Susan Ramer. She wanted to represent Kathryn.

Three weeks later, Ramer sold *The Help* (a novel about African-American maids working in white households in Jackson, Mississippi, during the 1960s) to Amy Einhorn books. It was published in 2009, spent more than 100 weeks on the *New York Times* bestseller list, sold 5 million copies a little more than two years after its release, and was made into a movie.

What worked for Kathryn will work for you too. For both writers and leaders, patience and perseverance are often the difference between success and failure.

Slow Down

Leadership guru John C. Maxwell says that leaders should take time to get to know their employees and that their approach must include a heavy dose of patience. Most often, company executives and those who aspire to be leaders are moving faster than the people they lead. They have more energy, more enthusiasm, more motivation. This, after all, is why you're reading this book—to learn how to pass on some of that energy and enthusiasm to your team.

To connect with your staff members, however, you need to slow down enough to walk at their speed. When you meet a colleague in the parking lot, in the hallway, or in the conference room before a meeting, allow yourself to postpone your agenda for a couple of minutes. Chat with that person. Ask about what's going on with the current project at work or the remodel at home. Give your staff member a chance to get to know you a little better. Yes, it takes patience and time out of your day to do this, but your staff will respond to you better and produce better results in the long run.

As your team's leader, you also need to remember that your staff has less information and less experience than you. When your employees take on a project that requires unfamiliar strategies or skills, you are the one who must train them and walk them through it. Maybe your team of accountants is being asked to meet with the media, a function it rarely performs. Maybe your sales staff is expected to provide a detailed written report on anticipated market changes for the next five years. Whatever the challenge, you can be sure that up-front patience on your part will increase the chances of your team's overall success.

Maxwell also says that the process is a little like parenting:

> The next time you need to get something done around the house, try doing it two ways. First, have your kids help. That means you need to enlist them. You need to train them. You need to direct them. You need to supervise

them. You need to redirect them. . . . Depending on the ages of your children, it can be pretty exhausting, and even when the work is completed, it may not be to the standard you'd like.

Then try doing the task alone. How much faster can you go? How much better is the quality of the work? How much less aggravation is there to deal with? No wonder many parents start off enlisting their children in tasks to teach and develop them but then throw in the towel after a while and do the work themselves.

Working alone is faster (at least in the beginning), but it doesn't have the same return. If you want your children to learn, grow, and reach their potential, you need to pay the price and take the time and trouble to lead them through the process—even when it means slowing down or giving up some of your agenda. It's similar with employees. Leaders aren't necessarily the first to cross the finish line—people who run alone are the fastest. Leaders are the first to bring all of their people across the finish line. The payoff to leadership—at work or home—comes on the back end.[1]

For too many managers, the alternative is to demand exceptional performance without giving employees time to adapt to the new task or system and to berate them if their performance doesn't meet expectations.

It reminds me of the story about a young woman whose car stalled at a stoplight. She kept turning the key and pressing the gas pedal, but she was so flustered that she couldn't restart the car. The light turned green, and there she sat, angry and embarrassed, holding up traffic. There was room for the car behind her to go around, but the driver chose instead to stay where he was and blare his horn.

In frustration, the young woman finally got out and walked to the car behind her. The man rolled down his window.

"Tell you what," she said. "You go start my car, and I'll sit back here and honk the horn for you."[2]

A patient approach is far more likely to lead to the results you want. That's true not just of your interactions with your staff, but also of your business plan for the future.

I know of a company chief executive who changed the structure of his organization almost annually. Departments and personnel were realigned, and objectives were redefined. He always looked for that winning strategy that would propel the company to new heights. Many of his ideas made sense. The problem was that he never gave the new systems time to develop. Innovations were abandoned before they had a chance to flourish. Employees spent as much time adjusting to new approaches as they did actually working.

Often, a patient, incremental approach is what's called for. Verizon Wireless was formed out of a merger of three cellular phone providers. The new leadership set a goal of resolving more customer issues at the first point of contact. Managers understood that this meant expanding the authority of callers and improving access to more systems that had been closely held by other departments. Rather than implement all the changes at once—perhaps upsetting employees who were already adjusting to the merger and even creating "turf wars"—managers moved toward the goal in baby steps. This strategy took longer to reach the goal than an immediate, comprehensive change, but it also prevented costly losses in productivity by stressed-out employees.[3]

As a leader, part of your task is to create a culture of patience within your team. It starts with you.

Psychologist Dr. Beverly Smallwood offers five tips on how you and your team members can develop patience:

➤➤ **Become more realistic in your expectations.** "Stuff happens," and the sooner we acknowledge that, the more accurately we can plan the tasks in our lives. Optimism is good, but unrealistic optimism about uninterrupted smooth sailing can sabotage the completion of important tasks. Expect and plan for delays, complications, and setbacks. You'll be better prepared if they happen, and delighted if they don't.

➤➤ **View setbacks as temporary.** Research shows that the most resilient people are able to view problems as temporary. They often use the adage, "This too shall pass."

➤➤ **Have the mentality of the problem solver, not the victim.** The theme song of people with the victim mentality is, "Gloom, Despair, and Agony on Me." They see themselves as unfortunate pawns of negative forces and other people who control their destinies. Problem solvers, on the other hand, look at negative situations to discover what they can do. They are able to distinguish the things over which they have control versus the things that they can't change. Within the conditions they face, they stay involved and active in doing the little things that make a difference. They work especially diligently in keeping their own internal reactions positive and constructive.

⟫→ **Reject bitterness.** Bitterness is the result of anger that is not resolved. It's a killer, psychologically, relationally, and physically. Bitter people are anything but patient. They have short fuses and overreact when even unrelated situations remind them of the person or event they resent. Resolve conflicts promptly, choose to forgive, and move on.

⟫→ **Remember your successes in other difficult situations.** When you find yourself in a mess that seems unending and you wonder if you'll ever make it, take heart. Remember that you've been in tough situations before, and you're still here. Recall times that looked impossible, but you found a way. Have faith that this time will be no exception.[4]

Here's another idea that should enhance a culture of patience at your company, as well as creativity: Encourage your employees to fail.

I'm told that the managers at a leading computer company have an unusual rule for their design team. When the time for evaluations rolls around, if any of the designers didn't come up with at least two failed projects in the previous year, they earn a reprimand. The talk managers have with the offending designer goes something like this: "You're being reprimanded because you're not thinking outside the box. We want you to be creative, to push yourself. We want you to risk trying things that may not work. That's where the innovative ideas come from. Don't be too proud to fail."

When you as team leader show patience for crazy ideas that don't work, your team is also more likely to offer creative solutions. Patience with failure leads to innovation and success. It's another way for you to inspire your people.

As you work on being more patient and developing patience within your team, give it time. In other words, be patient. You won't see the fruit of your efforts right away.

Have you ever walked through a field in summertime and felt those annoying cockleburs digging into your ankles? They're thin, brown weeds armed with dozens of sharp spines that attack your socks and eventually work their way into your skin.

Cockleburs are a nuisance, but they can also teach us a lesson. Inside their seedpods are several seeds that germinate in different years. The first seed may fail to sprout because of poor conditions, but the second seed is still waiting in the ground. When the next season arrives, this seed begins to open and grow. And if that one doesn't take root, there's still a third seed waiting for the year after that.

Your persistence will pay off. It may not happen in the first week, the first month, or even the first year. But you can have faith that patience in the workplace will eventually yield a bumper crop. The results for you and your team will be well worth the wait.

Insights for Inspiration—and Results

▶▶ The patience you show as a leader sets the tone for every future interaction you have with your team.

▶▶ When you create a culture that encourages patience, it improves the office environment and your ability to plan effectively for the future.

▶▶ Help your staff foster patience by setting realistic expectations for performance and projects.

▶▶ Encourage creative ideas that may fail. If you allow your team to test ideas that don't always work, you'll uncover the winners that lead to lasting success.

What Inspires People?
COMMUNICATION

9

> *The art of communication is the language of leadership.*
>
> James Humes

Author Jim Lange illustrates the importance of effective and specific communication with this made-up (I hope!) story from one of his books:

> A couple of rednecks are out in the woods hunting when one of them falls to the ground. He doesn't seem to be breathing and his eyes are rolled back in his head.
>
> The other guy whips out his cell phone and calls 911.
>
> He frantically tells the operator, "Bubba is dead! What can I do?"
>
> The operator, in a calm, soothing voice says, "Just take it easy. I can help. First, let's make sure he's dead."
>
> There is silence, and then a shot is heard.
>
> The guy's voice comes back on the line and says, "Okay, now what?"[1]

As a leader, you may think you're communicating effectively with your team, but what seems obvious to you may be interpreted quite differently by your employees. Whether the issue is instructions for a project, conflict resolution, performance expectations, or a statement about the future of the company, accurate communication is vital. And as we can see from the story above that a breakdown in communication between sender and receiver can quickly lead to disaster.

I am a professional speaker. Communicating is my business, and I take it seriously. Before I appear in front of an audience, I carefully plan what I intend to say. I attempt to memorize most if not all of my presentation. I want to own it. I give thought to each word, each story, and each joke so that my delivery is just right. I even consider how long I want my pauses to be.

I also ask myself about the overall effectiveness of what I've prepared. Will I be giving the members of my audience the information they need? Will they understand? Will they walk away encouraged and motivated? My goal is to hit a home run every time I speak.

There's no reason why you shouldn't adopt the same approach to communicating with your staff. Maybe someone in your organization has dropped the ball on an important task and it's up to your team to step in and fix the problem. You decide to call everyone together for a meeting. Don't walk into the conference room expecting to just wing it. Take a little time to think about what you want to say, how it will be best received, and how you can leave your team feeling encouraged and motivated.

Inspiration depends on effective communication. Let's get into it by exploring three communication targets every leader should aim for. Communication should be personal, precise, and persistent.

A Human Face

The National Aeronautics and Space Administration (NASA), started in the late 1950s, was organized into systems designed to meet specific challenges and needs. The scientists who dominated NASA believed that an exchange of computer-based information would be enough to keep the systems running smoothly. They soon discovered, however, that face-to-face interaction was critical to their success. Without continuous communication among the people assigned to various projects, questions about jurisdiction, direction, budget, personnel, and priorities bogged down the systems.[2]

Leaders have a tendency to take the easy road to communicating with their people. They send out an e-mail, memo, or report that describes what needs to be done, and then they figure that's enough. This kind of written information is vital. It can be enough in certain situations, but it is the personal touch that brings the most clarity to communication. When you physically meet with your team members to give them an assignment—or even better, speak to them one-on-one—you provide more than the basic facts. Your facial expressions and your tone of voice convey the significance of a project in a way that no e-mail or report can. Your physical presence allows your staff to ask questions that clear up confusion. Their insights can also give you valuable feedback.

There may be a better, quicker way to get the project done that never occurred to you.

Putting a "human face" on your instruction gives you the best chance of leaving your intended impression on your team. Whenever you rely solely on the written word, your message is open to interpretation. Sometimes those interpretations won't be anything close to what you had in mind.

Soon after General Tony Zinni was named commander of U.S. Central Command in 1997, the foreign minister of Qatar requested that Zinni agree to be interviewed by Al Jazeera television in the Middle East. Zinni, knowing that Al Jazeera usually portrayed America in a negative manner, felt initially that it was a bad idea:

> "Whether the interview is friendly or not," [the foreign minister] told me, "it's critical to put a human face on the American military in our region. If you don't," he continued, "you'll leave the communication of your image to those who will present it in a bad light. There's great skepticism about your reasons for being here. It's important for you to respond to these doubts; but even more important, you have to show who you really are."
>
> I reluctantly agreed to several interviews. Though they weren't easy, the questions and follow-ups were good and balanced. In one interview, for example, I was asked about how we accounted for possible collateral damage and the "moral" aspects of our actions in operational planning. This excellent question allowed me to describe the painstaking measures and risks we took to

ensure civilian safety and respect for religious and his-
torical sites. . . .

Later feedback indicates that my Al Jazeera inter-
views succeeded in showing America in a positive light.
The minister's savvy advice about "putting a human
face" on our military leadership was right on.

I did not regret the experience. It made me realize
that you can't let others define you or your organization.
The leader must step forward and give his organization
an honest and accurate personal presence. The days
of leading by decree and from the sanctuary of an oak-
paneled office are over.[3]

Face-to-face communication is a must for today's leaders. There is a challenge, however, that must be taken into
account when dealing with younger employees. Most young
people are used to working independently. They're also
highly comfortable with and heavily invested in technology.
They don't feel a need for personal interaction, often believe
meetings are a waste of time, and would prefer to conduct
their business by e-mail or texting.

This attitude goes against everything I've just said. So
what's a leader to do?

You must find a balance. Be aware that your younger staff
members may be impatient with meetings, so don't call them
too often or let them drag on needlessly. Send the e-mail that
gets your people started on a new project. But don't stop there.
Make it a point to follow up personally. Even a brief one-on-
one conversation can be enough to clear up misconceptions

and steer that person in the right direction. You can and should help younger employees understand the importance of face-to-face interaction.

Details, Details

Remember the redneck story at the beginning of the chapter? The 911 operator was not as specific as she could have been. Bubba's friend thought he was just following directions, but the result actually made matters worse.

We live in a fast-paced world. The temptation is to pass on the bare minimum of necessary information so that we can get back to doing what's "important." When we do, however, we run the risk of failing to communicate. In at least one study, poor communication was cited as the cause of poor performance 80 percent of the time. Often, the investment of extra time up-front to make sure a message is properly sent and received saves hours or weeks of trouble later.

It's equally important to choose words that convey exactly what we mean when we speak or write. The decision to change even one word for another can have a significant impact. A man, Jerry, was asked to eulogize the life of a friend who had just died. Jerry worked hard on his remarks. Just before the service, the departed man's wife made a request: "Jerry, I don't want this to be sad and depressing."

Jerry delivered his remarks exactly as he'd written them, with one exception. He took out the word "funeral" and replaced it with "celebration of life." That single change, small as it was, completely altered the tone of the ceremony.[4]

What does all this mean for you as a leader? You must be detailed and precise in your communications. You should communicate in a manner that you're sure your team will understand. And you must confirm that your intended message was received.

It's not enough to send a memo to your assistant and say, "Management is thinking about buying a phone system for the company. I need you to write a report about its pros and cons by Friday."

That statement is a start, but it leaves many questions unanswered. What is driving the look at a new phone system? Efficiency? Budget? Customer complaints? Are other options also being considered? What report format is preferred? Where is more information available? Who already has this system in place? Give your assistant the details if you expect a thorough job.

You also want to speak the language of your team. Socrates, as described in Plato's *Phaedo*, said that a person must communicate with others in terms of their experience. We should use language the receiver understands, such as farm metaphors when talking with a farmer. If you start throwing in technical terms about phone systems or management goals that your assistant has never heard before, your message won't get through. That's why it's wise to take a moment to put yourself in your employee's shoes before you pass on your instructions and expectations. Think about what type of communication he or she is most comfortable with.

Most people are primarily either readers or listeners. They absorb information most effectively one way and less so the other. When Lyndon Johnson assumed the presidency after the assassination of Jack Kennedy, he inherited Kennedy's staff. Staff members continued to write reports for their new boss just as they had for the previous one. But Johnson, unlike Kennedy, wasn't a reader. He was a listener. Their efforts were largely ineffective because Johnson was more comfortable gathering knowledge by the spoken word.[5]

The unique individuals on your team are divided into readers and listeners. That's why it makes sense to take advantage of both styles of communication when you need to get a message across. While you're at it, you might figure out which style works best for you and let your team know. You may find that your staff suddenly starts making a lot more sense!

Whatever the communication style you and your team prefer, it's also vital that you avoid overwhelming your audience. Boil down your message into bite-sized chunks that your people can digest.

A motivational speaker once sat in on a one-day leadership conference for a telecommunications firm. Using PowerPoint slides, management executives presented 138 "leadership imperatives" to attendees. It was too much information. As the speaker later noted, "I have a hard time remembering seven-digit phone numbers, much less 138 imperatives."[6] This company's leaders would have been wiser to choose only the key imperatives and emphasize those in their presentation.

A U.S. senator named Edward Everett was one of the most eloquent orators of his time. He spoke frequently to audiences across the country. Though skilled, however, Everett was also long-winded. On November 19, 1863, he gave a speech at the dedication of Soldiers National Cemetery in Gettysburg, Pennsylvania, that lasted nearly two hours.

Another speaker that day delivered a talk that was much briefer. In fact, it was only 10 sentences. Yet in those few sentences, U.S. President Abraham Lincoln imparted one of the most powerful and memorable speeches in U.S. history. Lincoln began with "Four score and seven years ago . . ." and concluded with ". . . that government of the people, by the people, for the people, shall not perish from the earth." In just over two minutes, his Gettysburg Address redefined the Civil War as a struggle for true equality for all citizens. When communicating a message, less is often more.

That concept applies to the actual words you use as well. Big words and phrases meant to impress are more likely to confuse. It's better to avoid too many corporate buzzwords. Don't talk about "monetization" and needing a "level set." Talk about making money and understanding. Don't use eight words when four will do. If you're writing an e-mail, read it to yourself, out loud, before sending it. Does it sound like a normal conversation? If not, it's time for a rewrite. You shouldn't sound like a robot. You should try to sound like you.

The last important step to remember is to find out if your message was received. Another advantage to face-to-face communication is that it's much easier to find out if your team is catching on to what you want. Simply ask team members to restate the goals and assignments you've communicated in their own words. It's a fantastic way to clear up misunderstandings and prevent problems before they happen.

Play It Again, Sam

It's been said that people will believe anything if they hear it often enough. As a leader, you're not out to brainwash your team, but you do need to realize that some messages take longer than others to sink in. Repetition can be your friend.

Jack Welch, the former General Electric CEO, talks about the urgency of communicating the company vision continuously to everyone in the ranks. Leaders who describe the vision only to their immediate colleagues and expect it to filter down to everyone else are usually disappointed. The message, if it's passed on at all, gets lost in translation.

According to Welch, one company that understands the power of persistent communication is Northwestern Memorial HealthCare. During an investment meeting, Northwestern's chief investment officer, Steve Klimhowski, couldn't help talking about the hospital mission to deliver excellent healthcare from the patient's perspective:

> He had examples of how employees at every level—including him, the investment guy—had transformed their work to fulfill the vision. He had been coached, for example, never to give outpatients directions to a location in the hospital, but to walk them there. At his performance review, Steve had been asked to list several ways in which he personally had improved the patient's experience at Northwestern Memorial. In fact, Steve's understanding of his role in achieving the mission, and his passion for it, were so real that after talking to him

for just five minutes, you could wake me in the middle of the night and I could tell you about it!

Clearly, Northwestern Memorial's leaders had communicated the hospital's vision with amazing clarity and consistency. And that's the point. You have to talk about vision constantly—basically to the point of gagging. There were times I talked about the company's direction so many times in one day that I was completely sick of hearing it myself. But I realized the message was always new to someone. And so, you keep on repeating it.[7]

Persistence should apply to more than the company vision. Any important message is worth repeating to your team members. If you communicate it often enough, they'll begin to understand that this is truly important.

A recent study found that managers "who are deliberately redundant as communicators move their projects forward more quickly and smoothly than those who are not." The study, conducted by Tsedal Neeley, assistant professor at Harvard Business School, and Northwestern University's Paul Leonardi and Elizabeth Gerber, was titled "How Managers Use Multiple Media: Discrepant Events, Power, and Timing in Redundant Communication." According to an article published by Harvard Business School, the study examined how managers in six companies across three industries (computing, telecommunications, and healthcare) persuaded staff members to meet their deliverables on time and on budget. Those who employed multiple methods to communicate the same message—e-mail, other forms of written communication, and face-to-face meetings—were the most successful.

According to the article, "Power, it turns out, plays a big role in how managers communicate with employees when they are under pressure. The research showed that 21 percent of project managers with no direct power over team members used redundant communication, compared to 12 percent of managers with direct authority. And 54 percent of managers without direct power combined an instant communication (via instant message or a phone call) with a delayed communication (e-mail), compared to 21 percent of managers with power."

The researchers found that those managers without power were "much more strategic, much more thoughtful about greasing the wheel" to get buy-in and to reinforce the urgency of the previous communication. While both sets of managers ultimately got the job done, it was the managers without power who moved their teams faster. "Managers with power spent more time on damage control after assuming an employee had finished the work," researchers found.[8]

Have I said this often enough to get across my point? It isn't your position or your authority that will push your team to action. It's repetition of the message.

Evaluation Time

One of the hardest tasks—and greatest opportunities—for a leader can be the performance evaluation. It is a chance to talk about where your team member is going as an individual and as part of your organization. It is a meeting where you can reconnect on goals and, if needed, reassign priorities.

Remember my love for basketball? I have an interesting and unique opportunity every so often to conduct some evaluations of my own within my favorite sport. I'm occasionally approached by parents who want me to serve as a personal basketball trainer for their son or daughter. My first step is always a series of drills: shooting, dribbling, defense, running, and jumping. Then I ask the parents, as well as the boy or girl, about goals. Do you want to play for the YMCA? A church league? The middle school, JV, or high school varsity team? Based on my evaluation and their goals, we set up a plan for getting them there.

Sometimes, however, the dreams of the family don't match the skills of the player. It's always hard when I have to say (as tactfully as possible), "I can see that your son is prepared to work and has a great attitude, but I'm afraid he just doesn't have the skill set to be a varsity player. But I do have some other ideas that may be helpful." It's better to be honest now than to offer false hope. The blessing is that if he redirects his energy into an area where he's more gifted, he has the chance to really excel.

The same is true of your employees. You need to be honest about how they are meeting or failing to meet your expectations. Their best chance of fulfilling their potential as part of a team depends on your frank feedback. An effective way to deliver bad or difficult-to-hear news is what I call a "reprimand sandwich." Start with a recap for both of you of what your employee is doing well. Then transition into the necessary conversation about where your employee is falling short and what specifically needs to change. Finally, end your talk with another positive by noting a strength or your team member's potential.

Your conversation doesn't have to be a downer. It can lead to unexpected solutions and improved performance, especially if you practice the listening skills we discussed earlier. And if things just aren't working out, it's better for everyone to get that out in the open sooner rather than later. You can help redirect your employee to another position in the company or someplace else where he or she can truly shine.

Fortunately, if you are a personal, precise, and persistent communicator, anything you say in an evaluation won't be a surprise. You'll have been sending these messages all along, and your team member will have been inspired to act on your comments. Strong leaders are strong communicators. They get results.

Insights for Inspiration—and Results

➣→ Face-to-face communication takes more time than an e-mail but may be more effective and efficient in the long run.

➣→ Make sure you include all the pertinent details when communicating with your staff and check to make sure your message was accurately received.

➣→ When communicating with your team, repetition can be your friend.

➣→ Use employee evaluations to inspire your staff, but be honest about areas that need improvement.

What Inspires People? 10
➤➤ INTEGRITY

A bby, age 16, was the proud owner of a new driver's license. She wanted the chance to show off her skills. She pleaded with Lori, her mother, for a chance to drive. Lori saw an opportunity to fill two needs with one shopping trip. She handed her daughter a grocery list and a hundred-dollar bill and sent her off to Walmart with an admonition to "be careful."

Abby arrived safely at the store. She checked her hair and lipstick and sauntered in. With the grocery list and single bill in hand, she maneuvered through the aisles, filling her grocery cart as she walked.

Soon Abby finished her shopping and was ready to pay for her goods. But her sense of accomplishment suddenly turned to panic. The hundred-dollar bill—where was it? Abby searched her pockets. She retraced her steps through the store. The money was gone.

Abby's eyes filled with tears. She ran to the customer service counter and wailed, "I lost my mom's hundred-dollar bill! She sent me in for groceries, and I lost it! She is going to be so mad at me!"

The customer service employees took Abby's name and phone number. There was little else they could do. Most likely, Abby's terrible mistake had already made someone else's week.

That evening, Abby was home with her mother. She hadn't been punished, but she was still terribly upset. Suddenly, the phone rang. It was a Walmart employee. Incredibly, a college student had found the bill and turned it in. In a moment, Abby's awful day was transformed. She and her mother were overjoyed by the student's unexpected example of integrity.[1]

Integrity matters to all of us. People in positions of authority—government officials, teachers, parents, and the boss at work—are especially on the hot seat. They are constantly observed and analyzed by the people around them. If they display deception, dishonesty, and selfishness, the men, women, and children they hope to influence will instead turn away. No one trusts a cheater and liar. No one wants to give their all for people who are only about themselves.

A leader of integrity, however, is a different story. The man or woman who not only talks a good game but also lives it out earns our admiration and respect. This is someone we want to be around. This is someone we can learn from. This is someone we will invest in.

At the corporate level and in your individual interactions with your team, integrity is everything. Your people will follow you anywhere if they know you are honest and trust-worthy. They will produce because they believe in who you are as a person.

Openness and Integrity

Human beings can usually tell instinctively whether some-one is open and genuine or deceptive and inauthentic. Our senses warn us when someone has a personal agenda that he or she is trying to hide. When that person is our boss, we hardly feel inspired to go the extra mile, to stay the extra hours needed to make projects truly excellent.

That's why, as a leader, it's so important for you to cul-tivate your honesty and openness. There's an undeniable link between truth, transparency, integrity, and trust. If your team members see you leaving out one of these traits in your interactions at work, the chain is broken. They'll turn away—or maybe even turn on you. Candid speech and transparent actions, on the other hand, are inspiring. They unlock com-mitment and creativity, bringing out the best in the people around you.

Joe Driscoll is a leader who believes in openness and in-tegrity. He spent 20 years of his career at Blue Cross Blue Shield of Massachusetts, where he was a senior vice presi-dent, before leaving to form a consulting practice. In 1998, he joined Private Healthcare Systems. Within a year, he took over as CEO and was charged with turning around a com-pany that was losing $1 million a month.

By 2006, when Private Healthcare was acquired by Multi-Plan, Driscoll and his colleagues had changed the company's culture and bottom line. The value of Private Healthcare had grown tenfold. The seeds of this success story were sown from the beginning of Driscoll's tenure, as he explains:

> If you're going to be open, then you've got to have integrity. They are inextricably connected. You can't be open and be misleading people, and they know that. When they know that there's integrity in management involved, it reinforces credibility and leads to real commitment to the corporate objectives.
>
> One of the first things I said when I got to Private Healthcare Systems was to tell everyone that this is going to be an open group of people. We're going to work together. We're going to respect each other, have full and complete discussions, be honest with each other, and then move forward to get the job done. I said that from day one. I knew it was the right thing, and I knew it because I had seen so many other companies not do as well as they could have because they were not open. I believe it absolutely has to begin at the top. And it didn't in the examples I saw previously in my career. A big part of it is seeing others and maturing and knowing I had made mistakes along the way by what I'd call perhaps a brash openness and learning to lead in an open way, by example and not by challenge.[2]

Driscoll promoted openness at Private Healthcare by admitting to mistakes and by encouraging all the employees in the company to offer feedback even if the topic wasn't their area of expertise. When the company was in the process of being sold, Driscoll implemented an "Ask the President" e-mail program which gave employees the opportunity to go to the top and get straight answers to their questions and concerns. Driscoll committed to answering every query within 24 hours and published the responses for all to see.

Driscoll's openness policy paid dividends. As he put it, "Belief in the integrity of the leadership team creates tremendous trust among all the employees. That trust will bring most employees to believe in the goals and objectives of the organization and then to commitment to the achievement of those goals."[3]

A Sense of Peace

Integrity is especially critical during your company's worst moments. Every organization faces a crisis sooner or later, but some seem to avoid catastrophes more easily than others. Maybe you can guess what they're doing right.

According to Jack Welch, the former General Electric CEO, it boils down to three preventive steps. The first is tight controls—disciplined financial and accounting systems with tough internal and external auditing processes. The second is good internal processes, such as rigorous hiring procedures, candid performance reviews, and comprehensive training programs.

The third is harder to measure but perhaps the most important of all—a culture of integrity.[4] A crisis that springs from shady dealings or just plain incompetence is a rare event when everyone in an organization shares similar and positive values.

Values were what Jim Hackett and Bill Marriott had in common when they met in the early 1990s. Hackett was the 39-year-old president of Steelcase, the office furniture company. Marriott was the 70-something founder of the Marriott hotel chain. They were from different generations, but they shared similar views on what was important in life.

Hackett admired the obvious sense of peace that Marriott enjoyed. Later that year, he met with his management team. "I talked about when a plane flies, it has what's called an altitude and attitude indicator," he said. "It tells you whether it's at the right height and whether it's level. And so I was looking for the metaphorical attitude indicator inside me. What would tell me that as I was pointing the company in the right direction, that I was still on the right plane, like Mr. Marriott had understood? What is that inside people that gives you peace? . . . You can be at peace knowing that you have values and know what they are."

Hackett's values and sense of peace were tested 10 years after his meeting with Bill Marriott. Steelcase had started selling a new line of products, with surfaces designed to be exchangeable between office cubicles and floor-to-ceiling walls. The company discovered, however, that the material was not up to fire standards when it was used for floor-to-ceiling walls.

It didn't seem like a major issue. "We had not had one damaged installation," Hackett says. "Our customers even called us and said, 'Oh, don't worry about it. What you're worried about, no one will ever have a problem.'"

Fire codes vary by municipality. In some areas, the product's fire-retardant level might have been enough to meet standards.

For Hackett, however, that wasn't good enough. He didn't want to just get by. He didn't want there to be any question about meeting fire standards. If he just let it go, he wouldn't feel at peace.

Steelcase recalled all the panels, replaced them with ones that met stricter fire codes, and took a $40 million write-off. Hackett and the rest of the company's executives lost their bonuses that year. It sent a clear message to every Steelcase employee: integrity mattered.

The postscript of the story involves the 9/11 terrorist attacks. When American Airlines Flight 77 struck the Pentagon, it also blasted into the improved, more fire-retardant Steelcase product. "It was determined," Hackett says, "with all the jet fuel and fire, if the new Steelcase material was not there, the fire would have spread in a far more disastrous outcome."[5]

Today, the employees at Steelcase sleep better knowing they did the right thing about a questionable product. They also know that they follow a leader who has values and integrity. I don't know about you, but I think that when they arrive at their office or factory each morning, they're a little more motivated to give their best.

Pizza on the Wall

When the company CEO displays integrity, it catches the attention of everyone in the organization. But what you do as the leader of your specific team will probably go even further in inspiring or discouraging the efforts of the people reporting to you.

I learned one of my first lessons on integrity in the workplace when I was 18 years old. I was a pizza-maker at a Domino's Pizza in Washington, DC. As you might expect in a kitchen full of young people, once in a while we messed up an order and made the wrong type of pizza. Those mistakes weren't passed on to the customer, of course. Instead, they became a "crew pie"—an occasional bonus that kept us hungry employees happy and well fed.

It didn't take long for me and a buddy to decide that instead of being happy and well fed once in a while, we could be that way most of the time. We started having more and more "accidents" with our pizzas, and our bellies got more and more full.

Then came the night that our manager caught on to what we were doing. She was furious. She flung a pizza against the wall (clearly wishing she could do that to us too) and yelled, "You will never, ever, do that again!"

We got the message. If we wanted to keep working there, it was time to start making pizzas the way they were supposed to be made.

Our manager's technique may have been a little rough, but it did get through to us. She wasn't going to let this slide. We wouldn't be allowed to eat our way through the night's profits. Integrity mattered to her. If we wanted to stay on the team, integrity had better matter to us too.

I saw a different type of integrity displayed when I was in graduate school when I was in my early twenties. My days of playing basketball at a high level were over, and I missed the competition. I still had a passion to test myself against others in athletic pursuits.

I decided to sign up for a tae kwon do program run by a well-known teacher in South Carolina. Not long after I enrolled, this teacher asked me why I was there. When I explained that it was for the chance to compete, the teacher got angry. He wanted students who were dedicated to the art, discipline, and history of tae kwon do. To be involved for competition, apparently, was a no-no.

From that point on, this teacher always picked me when he wanted to demonstrate a new move to the class. I was a human punching bag. I spent more time on the floor than the mats in the gym! Except for those demonstrations, he ignored me.

It stayed that way until a big tournament at the end of the year, the North Carolina state championships. Despite the inattention, I'd learned well and found myself in the finals of the men's adult sparring category. About 15 minutes before the match, my teacher came over, all smiles.

"Jeremy, how are you feeling today?" he asked. "No injuries from the earlier matches? Do you feel good, feel strong? Do you need me to help you get loose?"

I knew what was going on. I had his name on the back of my uniform. If I won the tournament, it would be great publicity for him. Suddenly, even though he hadn't said a word to me all year, we were all of a sudden best friends.

I lost respect for my teacher at that moment. Competition was offensive to him—unless he could benefit from it. As far as I was concerned, he didn't have much integrity.

I did end up winning, but soon after the tournament, I left his program.

Here's another example—I've heard more than one workplace story about sexual affairs within the office. In addition to the moral implications, that's also just bad business. In one case, a boss was having an affair with a woman in his department. He gave a raise to the woman and friends of the woman, but withheld raises from employees who weren't friends with his new partner. He was also slow to respond to the complaints of people who weren't in the favored circle. Needless to say, resentment was high and productivity low in that department.

People don't quit on organizations. They quit on people. If you are deceptive and dishonest in your dealings with your staff members, expect them to move on quickly. On the other hand, if you display integrity in every interaction with the members of your team, they'll be motivated to earn your praise and respect.

Your Word as Bond

We've talked about the differences between today's young employees and workers of past generations. The traditional values of security, loyalty, and playing by the rules are being replaced by the values of challenge, fun, independence, and opportunity. The generation Y staff member prefers making use of the latest technology and has less appreciation for meetings and face-to-face interaction.

Yet there are fundamental core values that bring all generations together. These are trust, openness, and honesty. In the short run, these are not always convenient qualities for a leader or a company to emphasize. In the long run, however, you, your team, and your organization will all see the greatest benefits from consistent dedication to integrity.

How do you know if you are consistently displaying integrity? Sometimes the shortest definition of integrity is to mean and do what you say. The boss who promises a raise or promotion and then changes his mind quickly loses respect. The manager who says she'll stand up for her team members and then blames them for an unexpected revenue loss will be leading an unhappy and unproductive group. Ask yourself if you follow through on your statements to your staff.

While you're at it, ask your team members for their opinion of your integrity. Promise that there will be no repercussions, no matter what they say—and mean it! When your word is your bond, you build trust.

Developing integrity is partly about discovering what you believe and then living that out. Bill Russell, the old Boston Celtics center, says his father and grandfather told him it's about finding a line inside you that no one can cross.

A Russell family story illustrated the point vividly:

> My grandfather worked for himself all his life, hiring himself out as a farm laborer, plowing people's fields and so forth. The most important thing to him, he always said, was education, making sure that young people who came after him would have wider opportunities than he had had.

Once, when he was a young man, he decided that he wanted to build a schoolhouse for young black children in the rural area of Louisiana where he lived. He went to a lumberyard to buy some wood to begin building. Somebody at the lumber store wanted the pile of wood my grandfather had just purchased. My grandfather wouldn't turn it over. A quarrel broke out. "We're gonna come and get you tonight, boy!" the customer threatened. When a car full of night riders pulled up to his house that night, my grandfather was sitting in a chair out front with a shotgun across his lap. "First man who steps across the line onto my property I'll shoot!" he shouted. When one of these guys then stepped past the boundary post of the front yard, my grandfather fired the shotgun—and the men took off. And somehow never bothered him again. The line they had crossed was that boundary line I had learned about. My grandfather was prepared to give up his life rather than let that line inside him be crossed.[6]

As a leader, you might consider where your own line has been drawn, and if it's where you want it to be. Sooner or later, your team will discover where your line sits and decide if it's in the right place.

India's Mohandas Gandhi knew where his line was drawn. Many consider him a great example of a man of integrity. A mother once brought her child to him, asking him to tell the young boy not to eat sugar, because it was not good for his diet or his developing teeth. Gandhi replied, "I cannot tell him that. But you may bring him back in a month."

The mother was angry as Gandhi moved on. She had traveled some distance and had expected the mighty leader to support her parenting. She had little recourse, so she left for her home.

One month later the mother returned with her child. She didn't know what to expect. Gandhi took the small child's hands into his own, knelt before him, and tenderly communicated, "Do not eat sugar, my child. It is not good for you." Then he embraced him and returned the boy to his mother.

The mother, grateful but perplexed, asked, "Why didn't you say that a month ago?"

"Well," said Gandhi, "a month ago, I was still eating sugar."[7]

A leader of integrity knows the right thing, says the right thing, and does the right thing, even when it's inconvenient. It isn't always easy. It can take a lifetime of reflection and practice. Yet when you commit yourself to becoming a leader who earns the respect and trust of your team, you will find your employees motivated beyond what you imagined, and your organization will achieve the successes of your dreams.

Insights for Inspiration—and Results

➤➤ Your people will follow you anywhere if they believe you are open, honest, and have integrity.

➤➤ Leaders and companies with integrity face fewer crises than those without.

➤➤ People don't quit on organizations. They quit on people.

➤➤ The shortest definition of integrity is to mean and do what you say.

➤➤ A leader of integrity knows the right thing, says the right thing, and does the right thing, even when it's inconvenient.

Epilogue

We've covered a lot of ground in this book. We have explored the characteristics that are essential to great leadership in the twenty-first century: passion, purpose, loyalty, a commitment to establishing a positive working environment and giving personal attention to each team member, understanding, patience, strong communication skills, and integrity.

What do leaders possess when they combine all these qualities? *Inspiration*. It is the key to unlocking the potential of your staff. It's the ingredient that enables you to lead your team to unprecedented success. Your ability to inspire makes you more than a manager. It makes you a *leader*.

During America's Civil War, at the Battle of Gettysburg, Pennsylvania, Colonel Joshua Chamberlain and his 20th Maine Regiment were assigned the critical task of protecting the Union Army's left flank. The Confederate Army repeatedly attacked the 20th Maine's position at the hill named Little Round Top, inflicting heavy casualties. With his regiment on the defensive and their ammunition nearly gone, Chamberlain realized that the Confederates were about to break through and surprise the rest of the exposed Union Army.

That's when Chamberlain chose an unexpected and audacious strategy. On the verge of defeat, he ordered his men to fix bayonets to their rifles and attack. The remaining men of the 20th Maine were inspired by Chamberlain and his brave gamble. Led by Chamberlain, shouting and raising their rifles, they charged down the hill. The Confederates were so surprised by the onslaught that they abandoned their positions and ran, allowing Chamberlain's men to regain control of the flank. Many have called this the turning point of the war.

Joshua Chamberlain understood the significance of inspiration. He was cited for bravery four times during the war and was later elected governor of Maine four times. He was a leader who earned the respect and trust of the people around him.

I hope this book has inspired you to become the leader you are meant to be. Study the principles in this book. Memorize them. Make them part of your daily routine at work. As you do, I think that you and your team will discover a wonderful truth.

Inspired people produce results.

Notes

Chapter 1

1. Mark Sanborn, *The Fred Factor* (New York: Doubleday, 2004).
2. Victor K. McElheny, "Edwin Herbert Land," The National Academies Press, http://www.nap.edu/html/biomems/eland.html.
3. Ibid.
4. Christopher Bonanos, "The Man Who Inspired Steve Jobs," *The New York Times*, October 7, 2011, http://www.nytimes.com/2011/10/07/opinion/the-man-who-inspired-jobs.html?pagewanted=all.
5. Ibid.
6. Brent Schlender, "25 Most Powerful People in Business," *Fortune*, July 11, 2007, http://money.cnn.com/galleries/2007/fortune/0711/gallery.power_25.fortune/index.html.
7. Adam Lashinsky, "Steve Jobs: CEO of the Decade," *Fortune*, November 4, 2009, http://money.cnn.com/2009/11/04/technology/steve_jobs_ceo_decade.fortune/index.htm.
8. Tim Barribeau, "Fortune Names Steve Jobs 'Greatest Entrepreneur of Our Time," *Fortune*, March 26, 2012, http://www.everythingicafe.com/fortune-names-steve-jobs-greatest-entrepreneur-of-our-time/2012/03/26/.

Chapter 2

1. "Passion at the Top—Apathy, Contempt for Managers," PR Newswire, January 21, 2005, http://www2.prnewswire.com/cgi-bin/stories.pl?ACCT=109&STORY=/www/story/01-21-2005/0002869774&EDATE.
2. Kevin Freiberg and Jackie Freiberg, "Passion: Finding It in Your Life, Building It in Your Business," Speakers Platform, http://www.speaking.com/articles_html/Drs.KevinandJackieFreiberg_854.html.
3. Hugh O'Doherty, "Help Workers Rekindle Passion in Workplace," *IndUS Business Journal*, December 15, 2007, http://www.indusbusinessjournal.com/ME2/Audiences/dirmod.asp?sid=&nm=&type=Publishing&mod=Publications%3A%3AArticle&mid=8F3A7027421841978F18BE895F87F791&AudID=EEB7C7075C2E462F969310BCC0CAA619&tier=4&id=B66E5FC5C4EE47CEA70CEE6F761F3131.
4. Lindsay Blakely, "5 Ways to Inspire Highly Passionate Employees," CBS News, March 30, 2011, http://www.cbsnews.com/8301-505143_162-40244115/5-ways-to-inspire-highly-passionate-employees/.

Chapter 3

1. Interview by Jennifer Robison with Roy Spence, "Your Company's Purpose Matters Now," *Gallup Management Journal*, February 12, 2009, http://gmj.gallup.com/content/114205/company-purpose-matters.aspx#1.
2. Seth Godin, *The Big Moo* (New York: Portfolio, 2005).
3. Ibid.
4. Ibid.
5. Joe Morrow and Vince Cavasin, "The Essence of Great Leadership: Creating Passion and Purpose in the Workplace," *Detroiter*, February 29, 2004, http://www.detroiteronline.com/index.php?option=com_content&view=article&id=894.
6. Niala Boodhoo, "Having a Purpose—Like Child Advocacy—Makes Work More Enjoyable," *Miami Herald*, September 6, 2009, http://www.miamiherald.com/business/careers/story/1220465.html.

Chapter 4

1. Anita Bruzzese, "Has Your Workplace Loyalty Gone to the Dogs?" *45 Things*, August 3, 2009, http://www.45things.com/2009/08/has-workplace-loyalty-gone-to-dogs.php.
2. Ibid.
3. Ibid.
4. Carmine Coyote, "Workplace Loyalty Cuts Both Ways," *Slow Leadership*, November 29, 2007, http://www.slowleadership.org/blog/2007/11/workplace-loyalty-cuts-both-ways/.
5. Margot Morrell and Stephanie Capparell, *Shackleton's Way* (New York: Viking, 2001).
6. Ibid.
7. Ibid.
8. Knowledge@Wharton, "Declining Employee Loyalty: Red Flag for Business," *The Fiscal Times* website, May 12, 2012, http://www.thefiscaltimes.com/Articles/2012/05/12/Declining-Employee-Loyalty-Red-Flag-for-Business.aspx#page1.
9. Stacey Thomson, "Cultivating a Good Employee/Manager Relationship," Disney Institute blog, January 5, 2012, http://disneyinstitute.com/blog/blog_posting.aspx?bid=19.
10. Tom Krause, "Loyalty from Leadership: Holding the Team Together," *Leader Values*, 2006, http://www.leader-values.com/Content/detail.asp?ContentDetailID=1116.

Chapter 5

1. Warren Bennis, *An Invented Life* (New York: Basic Books, 1994).
2. Warren Bennis, Holden Leadership Center website, http://leadership.uoregon.edu/resources/quotes.
3. "Lockheed Building 157," BuildingGreen.com, August 11, 2003, http://www.buildinggreen.com/hpb/overview.cfm?projectid=79.

4. Adapted from Loretta Lanphier, "Creating a Healthy Office Environment," Global Healing Center, http://www.globalhealingcenter.com /benefits-of/healthy-office-environment.
5. "Research Shows Healthy Workplace Environment Brings Business Benefits," http://www.squidoo.com/research-healthy-workplace -environment-furnishings.

Chapter 6

1. Tony Zinni and Tony Koltz, *Leading the Charge* (New York: Palgrave Mac-Millan, 2009).
2. John C. Maxwell, *Leadership Gold* (Nashville, TN: Thomas Nelson, 2008).
3. Bob Adams, *The Everything Leadership Book* (Avon, MA: Adams Media Corporation, 2001).
4. Tanveer Naseer, "A Lesson from School on Understanding Your Employee's Value," Leadership blog, March 21, 2011, http://www.tanveernaseer .com/lesson-on-understanding-employees-value/.
5. Zinni and Koltz, *Leading the Charge.*
6. Adams, *The Everything Book.*

Chapter 7

1. Shaunti Feldhahn, *For Women Only* (Sisters, OR: Multnomah Publishers, 2004).
2. Peter F. Drucker, *Management: Revised Edition* (New York: HarperCollins, 2008).
3. Keith McFarland, "Getting Personal with Your Staff," *BusinessWeek*, April 19, 2006, http://www.businessweek.com/smallbiz/content/apr2006 /sb20060419_388805.htm.
4. Tony Zinni and Tony Koltz, *Leading the Charge* (New York: Palgrave Mac-Millan, 2009).
5. Bob Carlisle, *Sons: A Father's Love* (Nashville, TN: Word Publishing, 1999).
6. Zinni and Koltz, *Leading the Charge.*
7. Alfred Lansing, *Endurance* (Wheaton, IL: Tyndale, 1999).
8. Noel M. Tichy and Warren G. Bennis, *Judgment: How Winning Leaders Make Great Calls* (New York: Portfolio, 2007).
9. Bill Russell, *Russell Rules* (New York: New American Library, 2001).
10. Drucker, *Management.*

Chapter 8

1. John C. Maxwell, *The 360-Degree Leader* (Nashville, TN: Thomas Nelson, 2005).
2. John C. Maxwell, *Winning with People* (Nashville, TN: Thomas Nelson, 2004).
3. Kristin Robertson, "Patience Is a Leadership Virtue," *KR Consulting*, June 2004, http://www.krconsulting.com/news_detail.aspx?news_id=24.
4. Beverly Smallwood, "How to Become More Patient," http://www.hodu .com/patient.shtml.

Chapter 9

1. Jim Lange, *Bleedership* (Mustang, OK: Tate Publishing, 2005).
2. Peter F. Drucker, *Management: Revised Edition* (New York: HarperCollins, 2008).
3. Tony Zinni and Tony Koltz, *Leading the Charge* (New York: Palgrave MacMillan, 2009).
4. Mark Sanborn, *You Don't Need a Title to Be a Leader* (New York: Doubleday, 2006).
5. Drucker, *Management*.
6. Sanborn, *You Don't Need a Title to Be a Leader*.
7. Jack Welch, *Winning* (New York: HarperBusiness, 2005).
8. Kim Girard, "It's Not Nagging: Why Persistent, Redundant Communication Works," Harvard Business School, April 18, 2011, http://hbswk.hbs.edu/item/6629.html.

Chapter 10

1. Julie Bryant, "A Story of Integrity . . . Unknown Student Thanked," Omnibus online, September 19, 2002, http://media.www.omnibusonline.com/media/storage/paper193/news/2002/09/19/TheGallery/A.Story.Of.Integrity.unknown.Student.Thanked-276472.shtml.
2. Sheila Murray Bethel, *A New Breed of Leader* (New York: Berkeley Publishing Group, 2009).
3. Ibid.
4. Jack Welch, *Winning* (New York: HarperBusiness, 2005).
5. Noel M. Tichy and Warren G. Bennis, *Judgment: How Winning Leaders Make Great Calls* (New York: Portfolio, 2007).
6. Bill Russell, *Russell Rules* (New York: New American Library, 2001).
7. George Ludwig, "Leadership Demands Integrity By Example," Frugalmarketing.com, http://www.frugalmarketing.com/dtb/integrity-by-example.shtml.

Index

About the Author

Inspirational speaker and author Jeremy Kingsley is one of the most sought-after speakers in the country. Since 1995 he has given over 2,000 keynote speeches to hundreds of thousands of people in the United States and around the world at corporate events, universities, music festivals, and conferences. His messages have reached millions through radio, TV, and the Internet. Jeremy is a master storyteller and connects with audiences through the perfect blend of humor, inspiration, and relevant principles to help each individual. He believes that inspired people produce results and is committed to helping people change, grow, and fulfill their personal and professional dreams.

World-renowned leadership expert Ken Blanchard said this: "Jeremy drives home one of my deepest principles in life and leadership—it's not about you. Let his words inspire you so that you can inspire others for the greater good."

Jeremy's early years were spent in the frigid winters of Wisconsin and his teen years in the politically charged environment of Washington, DC. In both places, he learned much about character, integrity, and effective leadership.

After playing three years on the high school varsity basketball team, Jeremy was named Conference Most Valuable Player his senior year and was recruited to play at the college level. He gave up the opportunity to play college basketball to attend Columbia International University in South Carolina, where he earned an undergraduate and graduate degree. Jeremy has the heart of an athlete and understands the importance of commitment, determination, and purpose.

Jeremy and his wife, Dawn, live in Columbia, South Carolina, with their sons, Jaden and Dylan. Jeremy enjoys running, basketball, and classic cars.

Would you like to have inspirational speaker Jeremy Kingsley, author of *Inspired People Produce Results*, speak at your company, organization, or special event?

Contact (803) 315-3042
www.JeremyKingsley.com
info@JeremyKingsley.com

You can also follow and connect with Jeremy here:

Facebook—Jeremy Kingsley
Twitter—@Jeremy_Kingsley